How To Speak A Sermon

(So That People Will Listen)

Larry Trotter

White Blackbird
BOOKS

Copyright 2022 by Larry Trotter

Published by White Blackbird Books, an imprint of Storied Communications.

All rights reserved.

No part of this publication may be reproduced, stored in a retrieval system, or transmitted in any way by any means without permission from the publisher, with the exception of reviewers who may quote brief passages in a review. Permission requests and other questions may be directed to White Blackbird Books at www.storied.pub.

Unless otherwise indicated, Scripture quotations are from the ESV Bible (The Holy Bible, English Standard Version), copyright 2001 by Crossway, a publishing ministry of Good News Publishers. 2011 Text Edition. All rights reserved.

Printed in the United States of America.

Edited by Doug Serven and Claire Berger

Cover by Sofía Vargas of Heavy.mx and Sean Benesh

ISBN-13: 978-1-951991-22-7

In Praise of How to Speak a Sermon

Great read for any pastor wanting to grow in the craft of preaching as an event. Many pastors I know feel intense pressure to have every word just right, which keeps them from being able to speak in the moment, pushing them to manuscripts and memorization. But others are so focused on the moment that content feels secondary and even like a distraction from the necessary entertainment. Dr. Trotter's book will push you to a balance of deep preparation—so right words and right content are available to you—and extemporaneous delivery, speaking biblical truth as an event with pastor and audience together with the Holy Spirit.
Dr. Tim Sansbury
Professor, Theology and Philosophy and Provost, Knox Theological Seminary

I believe, despite a staggering amount of evidence to the contrary, that the art of delivering a sermon that is rich in both content and form is still possible. This need is plainly evident today, yet as this study shows, history attests to a long struggle of combining the depth of serious exegetical and theological inquiry on the one hand with skillful, engaging, and persuasive rhetoric on the other. Though there are certainly exceptions, for many pastors this combination has become an either-or in which sermons leave congregants feeling either like they either survived a boring university lecture or were entertained with emotional storytelling. However, the two are not mutually exclusive, as

Larry convincingly argues. This book inspires the pastor-scholar towards greater eloquence and challenges the gifted orator to greater depth of content. Larry draws out clear, applicable principles from the great preachers in history and his own personal experience to guide today's preachers into effectively communicating the truth of scripture in ways that captivate attention and challenge the intellect. As such, *How to Speak a Sermon* is an important, fresh contribution that is very much needed for today's pastor (and congregations).
Dr. Scotty Manor
Professor, Historical Theology and President, Knox Theological Seminary

Larry Trotter practices what he preaches. I had the privilege of being mentored by Larry and sitting under his preaching for fourteen years, twice each Sunday—once in Spanish, and once in English! Each week, Larry opened God's Word to us with accessibility, clarity, power, and gospel-nourishment. This book reads like Larry's sermons in its engaging style, chock-full of wisdom and insight. If you are considering the pastorate or are a minister longing to improve your preaching ministry, let Larry speak to you through this accessible and cogent book. He will take some of the mystery out of expository preaching, and embolden you to engage more naturally with your congregation as you preach. Larry's preaching and Christ-honoring life have shaped me incalculably and inspired me to pursue the preaching ministry. May this book have the impact in your life that Larry's preaching has had in mine.
Rev. Keith Thomas
Pastor, Bridge City Fellowship, Portland, Oregon

Useful instruction is a rare gem, and perhaps the rarest is that instruction which informs not simply again, but more, each time it is read or heard. In *How To Speak A Sermon*, Trotter does not beg for application or plead a subjective case. By excellence of material and presentation, he elicits from his reader an automatic response of better methods and practices. The effect is unavoidable. I'll drink from this well deeply and often.

Rev. Jonathan G. Sargent
Pastor, Covenant Presbyterian Church, Russellville, Arkansas

Finally! The coaching I received from Larry is now being shared with preachers everywhere. This book comes from the heart and has a fresh, insightful, pithy approach with flashes of humor and keen wit. Pastors, seminarians, and the congregations they serve will greatly profit from this new resource.

Rev. Jeremy McKeen
Senior Pastor, The First Congregational Church of Hamilton, Massachusetts
Author, *The Model Sermon*

Studying homiletics under Dr. Trotter was one of the Lord's greatest blessings during my seminary years. I am thankful that his insight into the pulpit is now available to help equip and inspire pastors for generations to come. From the gripping introduction to the compelling conclusion, this book is both helpful for the pulpit and edifying to the soul. While most preaching books focus on organization and preparation, we tend to forget that far too often a well-organized and thoroughly prepared man delivers a sermon that simply falls flat on Sunday morning. Trotter helps us understand why and offers real solutions to this

common problem as he helps us rediscover the brilliance of what was perhaps the greatest age for homiletics in church history.
Rev. Wes Lauver
Pastor, Cornerstone Presbyterian Church, Palm Beach Gardens, Florida

For years, I benefited under Larry's preaching and tutelage. What he has practiced faithfully and effectively for years, he now makes available to all who would preach the Word with power. These are invaluable lessons for preachers at this current homiletical moment.
Rev. Steve Robertson
International Director of the Americas, Mission to the World

This book offers a wonderful blend of experience-based wisdom and careful, scholarly research. The relaxed, personal tone beautifully complements the numerous quotations from classical, historical, and contemporary sources. The author has done his homework! Larry Trotter also preaches what he teaches. His sermons combine rich insights gleaned from his text, logical flow, and an engaging, attention-holding delivery. It is a privilege to hear him, week after week. The novice preacher could have no better guide in learning to deliver spiritual food to his hungry congregation.
Dr. Constance Walker
Retired Senior Research Scientist, Duke University
Author, *Aldolphe Monod* (Bitesized Biographies), translator and editor of writings and sermons of Adolphe Monod

As a student and practitioner of homiletics, I walked away from Dr. Trotter's book grateful for his labors. I recommend this book not only to those who are just getting started in the practice of preaching but also to those who have labored long in the pulpit and are now looking for fresh insights and encouragement from a fellow-laborer. The examination of the historical correlation between extemporaneous preaching and the Lord's sending revival to the church was not only enlightening to read, but it also filled me with great hope for what the Lord may do in our time for the glory of his name and the upbuilding of his beloved church.

Rev. Dr. Brent Lauder
Senior Pastor, Providence Christian Church, Cape Coral, Florida

*To Sandy, Whitney, and Natalia,
who have heard most of my sermons
and liked many of them*

*and to the churches that taught me how to speak my sermons:
Glen Burnie Evangelical Presbyterian Church
Iglesia El Shaddai
Iglesia Cristo Redentor
Florida Coast Church*

Contents

Foreword by David B. Garner	xiii
Introduction	xvii
1. Now What Do I Do?	1
2. Why Public Speaking Is So Difficult	26
3. A Little Help From My Friends	36
4. How To Learn to Speak Well	70
5. Don't Try This at Home	108
6. What Happens When Preachers Speak	127

Foreword by David B. Garner

Carefully trained and wholeheartedly committed to faithfulness in preaching, many of us spend hours in the text—exegeting from the original languages, poring over commentaries, and creating theologically pristine sermons. At times out of a sense of duty but more often out of surging delight, we craft detailed outlines or full manuscripts, and then with scripts memorized or detailed notes on the pulpit before us, we address our congregations. On certain Sundays, we sense a unique unction of the Spirit. Sometimes we receive soul-boosting encouragement while shaking hands with our congregants at the end of the service. "Yes," they tell us, "Your words brought conviction, understanding of God's grace and the sweetest assurance!"

More often than we may admit the awkward encounters with saints at the back door communicate with unambiguous body language: "Thanks for trying, pastor. I'm sure you'll do better next week." Not that all our sermons are homiletical train wrecks, but all too often they do fall flat, in part perhaps because our pulpit ministry is commonly something more akin to theological lecturing than kingdom heralding. Yet our sermon delivery methods stubbornly persist. Some of us consign ourselves to our ruts. We are who we are. And after all, we deliver the goods of God to the people of God. What else can we do? At moments of ministry discouragement, we point our fingers at our hearers. "Yes," the voice in our head preaches, "their bobbing heads during our sermons expose their stiff necks."

But with good biblical reason and eyes of faith, we press on in preaching. Some of us even cling to that glimmer of hope that one day the Lord will release our inner Spurgeon. But as the years pass, such hopes for such impacting preaching progressively vaporize in the fading smoke of sermon after sermon.

In the midst of the homiletical highs and lows, if you are like me, you still read preaching books. I find that many of these books over promise and under deliver. Insights seem less than insightful, the assured impact less than impactful, and the radical new paradigm less than radical, less than new, and certainly not paradigmatic, at least for me.

So when Larry Trotter asked me to read his new work, I sighed. "Really, *another* book on preaching?" My spirit groaned until I picked it up and read it—all in *one* sitting. I was instantly glued. Page after page, my low expectations turned to high praise. Why? Let me offer five points (but no poem).

First, Trotter gives us something few others have done in recent generations. Most contemporary works on preaching attend to hermeneutics, the theology of preaching, or preaching styles. This book fills that much-needed space of preaching *method,* something Trotter clearly distinguishes from personality or style. Trotter is under no illusion that effective preaching depends on innate oratorical skill or word-smithing. He fully affirms the need for every preacher to study God's Word and to do so carefully. Effective preaching stands on God's Word and relies upon his Spirit. But Trotter also affirms what every preacher knows in his heart—that effective preaching requires attention not only to what we say, but how we say it. Self-conscious exegesis and theology must interface with a Spirit-inflamed, self-conscious methodology.

Second, Trotter reflects the strengths of a Reformed pastor-scholar. His broad and deep research satiates each page with clear and compelling insights. In fact, in its own right the impressive analysis of historic thinking on rhetoric and sermon delivery makes the book an imminently valuable read. Though it is short in length, the book is broad in reach, deep in wisdom, and high in usefulness. You will soon see what I mean.

Third, Trotter writes well, and I hope he writes more. Not only is the book structured coherently, but at a most granular level, his words invite and inform. Both wise and witty, his sentences land gently yet persuasively. He synthesizes and simplifies his vast research, and he artfully places gold nuggets of practical guidance within easy reach. The book is enjoyable to read.

Fourth, his writing is humble. Trotter communicates not as a self-promoting expert but as a servant among servants. He has spent his ministry preaching in diverse contexts and in *two languages*. Stretched by the demands of cross-cultural ministry, he possesses a deeply embedded grasp of the value of God's Word and its transcendent power in the pulpit. This rich multilingual backdrop, combined no doubt with the refining work of the Spirit in his heart, generate humble words from a humbled pastor. Trotter is not afraid to share his failures or his intermittent victories. He sincerely invites you to join him in submitting to God's Word, the Spirit, *and* the divinely appointed privilege to preach to the heart and not just to the head.

Fifth, convinced that merely reading or reciting is not the same thing as preaching, he argues persuasively for an extemporaneous approach to sermon delivery. And while contending for the benefits of this method, he does so with balance and grace. In fact, he encourages some preachers to give more attention to the other methods, including the writing of manuscripts. Trotter acknowledges that the Lord has gifted his church with a variety of preachers, none a cookie-cutter image of another. Balanced and honest, Trotter avoids the pitfall of turning his preferred method into an unqualified ministerial mandate. But at the end of the day, he convincingly urges preachers to speak rather than read, and he makes a compelling case for extemporaneity. It deserves our attention.

Sincere thanks to Rev. Dr. Larry Trotter for this helpful work. Those who listen to us preach will thank him too. After you join me in reading *How To Speak A Sermon*, you will never think about preaching in the same way again—precisely because you will think about it more often, more intentionally, and more perceptively.

Following Trotter's wise counsel, you will purposely prepare to preach more extemporaneously. You will *speak* a sermon so that people will listen. May King Jesus loosen our lips to proclaim his Word with kingdom impact!

David B. Garner, PhD
Chief Academic Officer, Vice President of Global Ministries, Professor of Systematic Theology
Westminster Theological Seminary, March 2022

Introduction

Preacher, has this ever happened to you? You identified your text carefully, studied it thoroughly, outlined it clearly, and developed its applications wisely. Sunday arrived, and you got up to preach. As you read the text, people were still shuffling around, and you had trouble getting their attention with your introduction. As you moved into exposition, somewhere around your second point, something began to happen both to you and to the congregation. Surprisingly, you saw connections and implications in the text that you had not previously noticed, and just the right words came to you to explain them. The look on people's faces changed, and your eyes locked with theirs in profound sympathy of feeling. You forgot about yourself and found an energy pouring through you almost as if you were passive. Preaching became effortless and the congregation was still as night. Nobody moved or made a sound. Your words flowed out of you effortlessly and almost uncontrollably, but they were few in number and hit home repeatedly. Then the dam broke. Your voice cracked as you spoke about Jesus. Your eyes welled up with tears. You paused to keep from breaking down entirely, but others in the congregation could not contain themselves. They wept openly, some convulsively. Someone shouted out, but it seemed appropriate, even in your normally staid church. Then the storm passed, and you finished out the sermon, completely exhausted but exhilarated. People approached you after the sermon with tears in their eyes, not commenting on your oratorical performance but about Jesus and his work. You groped for words of response, but the only ones you could find were, "Thanks be to God!"

Preacher, has this ever happened to you? You identified your text carefully, studied it thoroughly, outlined it clearly, and developed its applications wisely. Sunday arrived, and you got up to preach. You were especially satisfied with your preparation and the organization of the message. As you read the text, you stumbled over common words, garbling the last line. After you delivered your introduction, you realized that it didn't really introduce the theme of the text. You tried to recover with careful explanation of the text, but your ideas refused to flow, and your words became excessive. You found yourself repeating the same idea but adding no clarity on the second or third time around. A baby would not stop fussing, and two mobile devices went off, carrying with them the attention of the congregation. Several congregants were sleeping soundly. The fan seemed especially loud that day and the thermostat was too hot for some and too cold for others. You concentrated your attention on the text and the people as best you could. Then you decided to try vehemence to get their attention, increasing your pitch, volume, velocity, and vivacity but with no effect. You felt like you were speaking into the air, and you were wearing out both yourself and your hearers. You finally ended the sermon, which was longer than usual, feeling miserable. You wanted only to disappear, but you had to greet people. They politely thanked you for the sermon, both you and they implicitly knowing that little or nothing had passed between you and them that day. You went home, remorseful over having tried to fill in for the Holy Spirit.

Maybe you have had both of these experiences, maybe one, maybe neither. I have had both on the same day, preaching supposedly the same sermon to two different congregations. Most of the time when I preach, my experience is somewhere between these extremes, but I highly value both of the extremes because they remind me of what I am doing. I am speaking words born in the moment from a position of derived authority. I am utterly dependent on the Holy Spirit *and* on the congregation for the effectiveness of the sermon. I am performing what looks like a monologue, but for it to be successful it must become a dialogue. I am giving myself over to the congregation and am at its mercy. I face the possibilities of soaring or crashing. Something extraordinary may happen that day. God may break through to the congregation and to me. He will surely speak to us as long as I preach his Word.

What am I doing? I am preaching, preaching extemporaneously, preaching with thorough prior preparation and trying to cast off unhelpful restraints. This activity is an art, but it is not artificial. It expresses one of the most amazing aspects of being God's image. He created by speaking, and we imitate him. We commune with each other around God's Word through the medium of speech. Through our speech, God creates things—community, faith, repentance, salvation, joy, commitment.

This book is about the oral art of preaching. In addition to the Bible, it comes from three main sources: classical rhetoric, eighteenth- and nineteenth-century homiletics, and my experience. In a preaching course when I was a seminary student, Dr.

Timothy Keller gave us a bibliography that included Robert Lewis Dabney's *Lectures on Sacred Rhetoric*, which I read early in my first pastorate. I concluded that Dabney was a unique homiletical genius who captured the essence of preaching. The only word I could find to describe his insights was that he grasped the *romance* of preaching. I'm not sure that it is the right word, but Dr. D. Martyn Lloyd-Jones used it to describe his own experience of preaching.[1] It might be better to call it the *spirituality* of preaching, referring to the work of the Holy Spirit in preaching.

When I got the itch to do a doctorate (in part to help me through midlife), I focused my research on Dabney's work. As I got into the research, I made the disappointing discovery that Dabney was not a unique genius.[2] He was simply an exceptional product of his age, but what an age for homiletics! Three rhetorical strains coalesced beautifully: the biblical tradition of expository preaching dating back to Ezra, the classical rhetoricians like Aristotle and Cicero, and the British and French Enlightenment homileticians. It was the age of Charles Spurgeon in England, of Alexandre Vinet in Switzerland, Adolphe Monod in France, and of the Virginians John Broadus, Archibald Alexander and his son James. They examined and debated methods of sermon delivery, which was a hot topic, perhaps for the last time. Therefore, I turn to these people in order to learn how to preach a sermon, that is, how to *speak* a sermon.

How did I begin to learn how to preach a sermon? I made a few weak attempts to teach during university days, when I was testing a possible call to the ministry. At seminary, I received surprisingly little instruction on how to preach a sermon. There seemed to be an assumption that seminarians knew how to structure a sermon and how to speak in public, so the focus was mostly on exegesis of the text. In this book, I will tend to do the opposite—to assume instruction in exegesis and focus on how to preach a sermon. My best early training in sermon delivery was on the corner of Broad and Olney in Philadelphia, where some seminarians weekly (and weakly) tried our hand at street preaching. I'm quite sure our methods were not evangelistically effective, but it was where I learned to order my ideas beforehand, to be concise, and to try to let myself loose, three practices I've attempted to maintain ever since.

A few years ago I read a book on sermon preparation called *Unashamed Workmen: How Expositors Prepare and Preach*, in which ten contemporary preachers opened up their sermon workshops to explain how they prepare and deliver their sermons.[3] In addition to the helpful tips I picked up and warnings I hope to heed, I was struck by a couple of facts. One, all preachers have their own way of preparing and delivering sermons. Two, we all tend to think our way is best because it works best for us. To their credit, only occasionally did some of the contributors make absolute statements about aspects of preaching that are more personal than biblical. For the most part, they modestly described to others their practices, recognizing that gifts and contexts differ. I hope to maintain this posture when it comes to styles, differences, gifts, and cultural contexts.

At the same time, I want the present work to be more than my opinion or recommendations but rather, interaction with some of the best rhetoricians and homileticians of the ages. If there is anything unique about this offering among recent homiletics books, it is the constant attention to the orality of preaching, to the rhetorical act of speaking a sermon. In the West, we talk about *writing* a sermon and give assignments to students to *write* sermons. After the invention of the printing press and until the advent of audio recording technology, it was also common in the West to *read* written sermons. In other parts of the world, such an idea would likely be met with puzzlement. They might ask, "Isn't a sermon something that is preached and heard?" As we will soon see, most of the best homileticians recommended writing, but they did not suppose that the end result of writing is a sermon. A sermon is what happens when preachers speak God's Word to the gathered assembly. After all, "*faith comes from hearing*" (Rom. 10:17).

Although I am going to recommend extemporaneity in sermon delivery, I do not want to pick a quarrel with or denigrate those who use other methods. In fact, I will try to encourage some to push themselves toward greater freedom in their deliveries *and* warn others against too much freedom. My main audience is not so much those preachers who are already settled in a method effective for them but those who are learning to preach or who teach others to preach. I deeply value my ministerial training, but I would have benefited from more instruction in how to *speak* a sermon, which is what I hope to offer here.

I fear someone might read this book, then hear me preach some day, and wonder why my practice falls so short of my ideals. James W. Alexander (a most eloquent preacher whom you will meet in Chapter 3) comforts me with his confession:

> If long experiment, innumerable blunders, and unfeigned regrets, can qualify any one to counsel you, I am the man; for all my life I have felt the struggle between a high ideal and a most faulty practice. But what I offer with an affectionate

desire for your profiting is derived rather from the successes of others than from my own failures.⁴

Similar was the terse comment of a minister who had graduated from my seminary fifty years before I did and had the opportunity to say something at our graduation ceremony. He simply said, "I think I have not yet preached a very good sermon." Likewise Lloyd-Jones quoted the great Southern Presbyterian preacher James Henley Thornwell, who was even harder on himself: "My own performances in this way fill me with disgust. I have never made, much less preached, a sermon in my life, and I am beginning to despair of ever being able to do it. May the Lord give you more knowledge and grace and singleness of purpose."⁵ All of these preachers hit on the same idea—the more exalted our understanding of preaching, the lower our estimation of our own attempts to preach. I am thankful that Lloyd-Jones followed Thornwell's despairing self-evaluation with a word of encouragement: "Any man who has had some glimpse of what it is to preach will inevitably feel that he has never preached. But he will go on trying, hoping that by the grace of God one day he may truly preach." This is my prayer for my fellow preachers and for myself, that one day, we will truly preach.

---

1. D. Martyn Lloyd-Jones, *Preaching and Preachers* (Grand Rapids, MI: Zondervan, 1971), ch. 15.
2. Although I focused my research almost exclusively on Dabney's sermon delivery method, I also learned about Dabney's life and views, including his embittered defense of race-based slavery after the Civil War. For a balanced evaluation of Dabney, see Sean Michael Lucas' *Robert Lewis Dabney: A Presbyterian Life* (Phillipsburg, NJ: P & R Publishing, 2005).

3. Rhett Dodson, ed., *Unashamed Workmen: How Expositors Prepare and Preach* (Tain, Scotland: Christian Focus Publications, 2014).
4. James W. Alexander, *Thoughts on Preaching,* 1864 (Carlisle, PA: The Banner of Truth Trust, 1975), 154.
5. Lloyd-Jones, 99.

Chapter 1
Now What Do I Do?

If you are a preacher or aspire to be one, people will ask you in sincerity or in jest: "What do you do all week?" Although it is easy for preachers to be irritated by this question and respond defensively, we need to recognize that much of what we do to produce a sermon is invisible to the congregation. The people see and hear only the final step—sermon delivery, the topic of this book. However, devoted preachers know that there are many earlier steps that we take mostly by ourselves in communion with God and his Word.

All preachers develop their own approaches to sermon preparation, but common steps include:

- Studying the Hebrew or the Greek of the text and comparing translations.
- Analyzing the syntax of the text to understand how all of its parts fit together.
- Outlining the text itself.
- Viewing the text in the light of its immediate and

larger contexts to identify its redemptive-historical themes that lead to Christ.
- Making a homiletical outline that will facilitate preaching and hearing.
- Consulting the best biblical commentaries and modifying ideas in the light of their research.
- Filling out the outline, making sure the thoughts flow from the text and in a logical order.
- Including culturally relevant ways to illustrate the points that most need explanation.
- Using knowledge of the congregation to drive home helpful applications of the text.
- Developing a crystal clear conclusion and adding an engaging introduction.
- Praying throughout the process.

Let's assume that you walked through many of these steps. Then the Lord's Day arrived, and the time came for you to preach. You stood up, read the text, prayed briefly, and then started to say some words. Now, I want to ask, where did the words come from? The three possibilities were:

- You stored them previously in your head and recited them from memory.
- You read them off of a piece of paper or an electronic device.
- You invented them in the moment.

Maybe I should not ask about the origin of the *very first* words of the sermon, because many preachers treat the opening and closing words differently than they do other parts of their sermon, as I also recommend. Better to ask about most of the other words that you spoke in your sermon. Where did they come from? The three options listed above were the three methods that the eighteenth- and nineteenth-century homileticians analyzed and debated and practiced. They were reciting, reading, and extemporizing.

Impromptu Preaching

By the way, there also were (and are) so-called impromptu preachers who preached without preparation, but I do not plan to deal with their method except to note a few things. First, every preacher *must* be able to preach impromptu, because some circumstances will demand it, like hastily organized funerals, or when the scheduled preacher gets sick, or on occasions when someone asks the pastor to "say a few words." We should not miss out on such opportunities for usefulness by not having something excellent to say. Second, impromptu is generally not a good way to preach on a regular basis because careful exegetical work is necessary to mine the depths of Scripture. Third, dedicated and experienced pastors simply cannot truly preach impromptu, that is, without prior preparation, because they have been preparing constantly for years. They have already trained their minds to analyze texts automatically and to organize their explanation logically, and they have already done exegetical work on much of the Bible. While there may not have been much specific prior preparation for an impromptu event, pastors' entire lives of preparation enable them to preach clearly and carefully when called upon to do so at the spur of the moment. What appears as impromptu is the result of decades of mental and spiritual discipline.

I had the privilege of overlapping one semester with Dr. Edmund Clowney at Westminster Theological Seminary before he moved on. One day we were gathered for chapel when the appointed speaker apparently did not show up. Then someone whispered to Dr. Clowney, reminding him that it was his turn to preach, so he got up and, once he recovered from his embarrassment, delivered an amazingly cogent and powerful sermon from some obscure Old Testament text. I was stunned, wondering how in the world he could do that. After decades in pastoral ministry, I now know—he had spent many years preparing constantly in order to be always prepared. All preachers need to be always prepared.

Note that there is some difference of nomenclature in the literature. Some, like Charles Spurgeon and Charles Hodge, used the term "extemporaneous" to mean what I am calling impromptu, speaking without prior preparation of the content. Etymologically speaking, they are correct, since *extempore* is Latin for "out of time" or "without time." However, the majority of the nineteenth-century homileticians tended to use the word "extemporaneous" to refer to delivery that happens spontaneously without the prior selection of most of the words, which is how I am also using it.

Memorization and Recitation

Returning to the three main methods, recitation is when a preacher writes out a full manuscript, commits it to memory *verbatim*, and recites it to the congregation. In our day, there are very few reciting preachers, in part because of our relative mental laziness in comparison with our forebears. Why bother to remember things when we can look them up online? However, this used to be a common method, and it is not quite as difficult as we might imagine. Although I am far from recommending it, *memoriter* preaching has some advantages.

John Broadus, the most systematic and thorough of the nineteenth-century authors on homiletics, summarized the advantages of preparing a complete manuscript to be recited or read:

- "Writing greatly assists the work of preparation, by rendering it easier to fix the mind upon the subject."
- "Besides, writing a sermon compels to greater *completeness* of preparation."
- "Still further, writing serves to secure, in several respects, greater excellence of style."
- "The written discourse can be used on subsequent occasions."
- "The sermons remain for publication, if ever that should be desirable."
- "And then the practice gives facility in writing, which in our day is a highly important means of usefulness."[1]

He added that reciting from a memorized script has the additional advantages of truly being a kind of speaking and of developing the memory.[2]

However, Broadus went on to deliver a scathing critique of recitation, because it does not allow for the correction of errors, new insights, or "new shape and color to the thoughts," because it shackles the mind, because it consumes much time in preparation, because it fills the preacher with "the painful dread of failure," and because "the delivery of what is recited must always be more or less artificial."[3]

According to Dabney:

> The main objection to this method may practically be summed up in a single question: How deficient must that man be in the mastery of his mother-tongue, who judges it necessary to replace that attainment (which should be so fully the orator's) by an expedient so toilsome and injurious?[4]

In his posthumously published *Thoughts on Preaching*, James W. Alexander included the following gem:

> Memoriter Discourse—When Pompey the Great was going from the vessel to be murdered, he spent his time in the little Egyptian boat, in reading a little book in which he had written a Greek oration, which he had intended to speak to Ptolemy.[5]

Alexander offered no explanation for this thought, but apparently he considered that Pompey's fate typifies what happens to those who recite their orations.

Because very few memorize and recite their sermons these days, it is not necessary to beat this already dead horse. However, before moving on to the two more common methods, let me recommend recitation or something close to it in a few situations, such as the first words of the sermon and the last. The first words of the sermon are crucial because you probably do not have everyone's attention yet, and you need to get it. If you can capture it with your very first words, then you have a better possibility of holding it during your entire discourse. Therefore you must craft your opening lines well and deliver them with certainty. One way to do this would be to write them out and read them, but the introduction is no time for people to be looking at the top of your head. The other possibility is to memorize them and recite them. You need not worry much about forgetting them, because most memories can hold a sentence or two for the few seconds necessary to repeat them accurately and naturally. Also, if the idea is clear and some of the key words premeditated, you will be able to speak an excellent sentence without exactly reciting it. Although I do not write out my sermons (more on this later), I do write out my introductions and conclusions in paragraph form.

Also, I generally compose my introduction after doing all my other sermon preparation work, since I have to know first what it is I need to introduce. Cicero's character Antonius followed this same practice:

> All these things being duly considered, it is then my custom to think last of that which is to be spoken first, namely, what exordium [introduction] I shall adopt. For whenever I have felt inclined to think of that first, nothing occurs to me but what is jejune [simplistic], or nugatory [useless], or vulgar and ordinary.[6]

Managing the introduction is like shifting with a manual transmission. The hardest part to make smooth is the transition from a full stop to forward movement in first gear. Novice drivers often stall the car at this point or move forward with violent jerks (I do not mean that other passengers in the car are violent jerks but that the car's movement is violently jerky). Once the driver avoids stalling the car and gains some momentum, the shifting up and down is easier. The first words of the introduction are like going from a full stop to initial forward movement. Start well, and the other transitions of the sermon are more likely to go smoothly.

The other part of the sermon to write out and commit to memory is the conclusion, especially the last words. Concluding a sermon is like landing an airplane. Most travelers know the great difference between a smooth landing and a bumpy one. Many also know the experience of getting near the airport and having to circle in the air until landing conditions are adequate on the ground. Some may have even experienced an aborted landing, with the plane touching down and suddenly having to pull up again. Few have experienced an emergency or crash landing.

A well-designed and executed conclusion is a smooth landing that brings the whole discourse to a close with the right words to make it stick in the minds and hearts of the hearers. Many conclusions are more like bad landings. After repeating the same idea several times, some preachers run out of fuel and finally just stop talking (to everyone's relief). Perhaps they touch down once beautifully but then decide to take off again on another little side trip. Maybe they bounce through the conclusion with multiple stopping points, never really achieving any height after the first false ending. Better to craft the concluding words with care and deliver them with ease.

Another image is of gymnasts trying to "stick the landing" by taking no extra steps. We preachers need to stick our landings, taking no hops or bobbles after we have reached our destination.

I have to admit that some of my best conclusions have surprised me by coming to me as I delivered them. In these cases, I abandon my script and go with the flow of thought. On very few occasions, a better introduction comes to my mind as I am about to preach, and I use it. However, this sort of spontaneous adaptation is much more likely to be appropriate in the conclusion than in the introduction, because the preacher has already warmed to the subject, developed and applied it, and is so full of the text by the end of the sermon that something surprisingly better is more likely to burst out then.

There may be a few other places in the sermon when the preacher will want to commit particularly apt phrases or precise explanations to memory in order to say them just right. These generally occur during crucial parts of the sermon, so it is better to be looking at the people than at the pulpit. There are also special occasions that call for elegance, conciseness, and polish that can best be achieved by crafting beforehand and delivering from memory. For example, our church in Guadalajara, Mexico had a Good Friday service with each of seven preachers delivering a four-minute meditation on one of Christ's sayings from the cross. One year I decided to memorize and recite the brief text and the brief meditation. That way, I would be able to speak just the right words and look at the congregation the whole time. It was a good exercise for me and proved effective, but I found myself more nervous than usual beforehand, and I blanked briefly during the recitation, provoking a moment of internal alarm. I was able to recover without anyone noticing, but I got a brief glimpse of the homiletical equivalent of Pompey's fate.

Writing and Reading

A second and more common method of preaching a sermon is to write out a full manuscript and to read it to the congregation. I have friends and acquaintances who preach this way, some of whom regularly address larger crowds than I ever have. If their churches have multiple services, the sermons in each service are exactly the same, word for word. Also, every word is in its place, the vocabulary is elevated, the phrases are beautifully crafted, the length of the sermon is completely predictable, and the manuscripts are available for the public to read and study. Some of these sermons appear later as books for others to enjoy for generations. We can all be thankful for complete manuscripts of preachers of earlier years.

We have already heard Broadus on the multiple advantages of having a complete manuscript to recite or read, and he added one more advantage of reading in particular:

> As regards the delivery of the sermon, this method has the advantage of placing the preacher more at his ease, both before and during delivery. Having the sermon written, he will be preserved, and knows that he will be, from any utter failure. It is a great relief to escape the tremulous and often distressing anxiety which one is apt otherwise to feel. The preacher who means to read, has a far better chance to sleep soundly on Saturday night. It is also an advantage to be collected and confident while delivering the sermon, rather than oppressed by nervous solicitude, or driven wild by uncontrollable excitement. Some preachers find that reading saves them from an excessive volubility, or an extreme vehemence which otherwise they find it hard to control; and very many fear that without

the manuscript they would be utterly crushed by the dread of breaking down.⁷

He then went on to name several disadvantages of reading sermons, including:

- It trains preachers to think only as fast as they can write instead of as fast as they can talk.
- Preachers can use elegant writing to give the impression of thorough exegetical preparation. In other words, the sermon may sound good but say little.
- The mechanics of writing consume much of the preacher's time.
- Writing binds preachers to the first plan they conceive, because it is too much trouble to write it all over following another plan (a disadvantage partially overcome by composing with a computer).
- "This method also deprives the preacher's thinking of the benefit of all that mental quickening which is produced by the presence of the congregation."
- "As to delivery itself, reading is of necessity less effective, and in most cases immensely less effective, for all the great purposes of oratory, than speaking."
- "It should be added that reading is more injurious to the voice."
- "Yet the manifest tendency, and the common result of habitual reading, is to make one dependent and timid."⁸

Dabney's critique was more categorical when he

pronounced:

> Reading a manuscript to the people can never, with any justice, be termed preaching. Even if the matter and style are rhetorical, the action cannot be, but it is almost impossible that the structure either of thought or language should be such, when the invention is performed in solitude and at the writing-desk.[9]

When I listen to the best of preachers who read their manuscripts, I am amazed at their ability to make their reading sound almost like normal speech. According to Dabney, the best reading preachers have developed the ability to write in a rhetorical manner, which he recommended and approved. However, the thing that unnerves me when I am listening is that their reading sounds *almost* as if they were actually speaking to me. It leaves me wondering why they do not just go ahead and speak to me if that is the impression they are trying to make. Broadus anticipated this unsettling effect when he counseled manuscript readers not to pretend to be speaking but rather to aim to read well.[10]

If the best manuscript readers have mastered the art of reading in an oratorical style so as to leave me only slightly unnerved, the less skilled ones leave me downright agitated. I heard one preacher who alternated between reading *verbatim* some sections of his sermon and extemporizing other parts. The combination was jarring, since the extemporized parts sounded exactly like a human being speaking to other human beings about a subject of vital interest to all present, precisely because that is what they were. The read parts sounded like roaring. I assume that the extreme artificiality of the reading was overcompensation, an exaggerated attempt to make the reading sound like speaking. At least he had the kindness to give us breaks from the excessive vehemence by looking up periodically and speaking to us in a natural way. Others are not so kind.

For a homiletics course I taught in Mexico City, I had students give brief oral explanations of reading assignments. One student stood and read a solid report, looking at his manuscript the entire time and boring the rest of us exceedingly. After he finished, and at the risk of exposing him to embarrassment, I approached him, took away his manuscript, told him to tell us about the reading assignment, and sat down again. My gambit paid off. It was as if someone had passed a magic wand over the young man. Without losing anything in terms of content, he explained the reading assignment to the class in an orderly and animated manner, keeping our attention and engaging us with natural speech, eye contact, and movement. He had gifts for speaking but simply needed someone to let him loose.

I also had an experience in a seminary chapel service that helped to shape me. That semester I was taking a sermon delivery course with Dr. Keller, so I asked him if I could preach my required sermon not in the classroom but in a chapel service, to which he agreed. (That way, I could impress the whole seminary and not only my few classmates.) My manuscript consisted of seven or so handwritten and numbered pages written in paragraphs. I began decently enough but somehow got my pages out of order and became completely confused in front of the seminary community, including fellow seminarians, the president, several professors, and Dr. Keller, who was grading me. His conclusion was that it was the worst he had ever heard me preach. I'm sure I've preached worse sermons since then, but he didn't have the displeasure of hearing those.

Archibald Alexander, the first professor of Princeton Seminary, had his own defining moment. He recorded:

> My next sermon was preached at Charlestown, from the text, Acts xvi. 31, "Believe in the Lord Jesus Christ, and thou shalt be saved." I had prepared a skeleton of the sermon and placed it before me; but the house being open, a puff of wind carried it away into the midst of the congregation. *I then determined to take no more paper into the pulpit*; and this resolution I kept as long as I was a pastor, except in a very few instances.[11]

I cannot say that my miserable chapel sermon was as determinative of my future method as was Alexander's experience, but it has remained with me as a warning not to have more than two, or at most three, pieces of paper in front of me when I preach. It is, after all, difficult to get too hopelessly befuddled when there are only two sheets to confuse. Others could take away equally legitimate lessons, like numbering the pages more clearly or stapling them together in order. My particular takeaway led me in the direction of trying to develop extemporaneous ability.

In Chapter 5, I will reverse myself by recommending fuller manuscripts for certain preachers. However, before I leave this method, let me do for reading what I did for recitation by recommending certain parts of the sermon that are best read. For example, while quotations should be kept to the few that truly help explain or illustrate a point, it is generally best and most natural to read them. Similarly, statistics or complex facts usually require reading. In addition, especially complicated or difficult points lend themselves to careful prior editing and reading in order to get them just right the first time. In these cases, preachers should not try to disguise the fact that they are reading what they wrote. All will understand that they are reading a section, which will communicate to the congregation the seriousness and care with which they developed the ideas. Although I am about to recommend the third method, extemporaneous preachers do well to use recitation and reading judiciously in their sermons to give their hearers the best of two worlds—careful previously written thought and spontaneous utterance.

Extemporaneous Speaking

Extemporaneous preaching has been defined in various ways, and it does not primarily have to do with the prior use one makes of writing or the presence or absence of written notes in the pulpit. Some extemporaneous preachers like Dabney and Broadus insisted on the importance of writing, while James Alexander considered it optional.[12] With his typical thoroughness, Broadus gave a range of activities that can be called extemporaneous preaching:

- Preaching without prior preparation (which I am calling impromptu)
- Preparation of the thoughts without premeditation of the language
- Speaking with the aid of an outline (which some of the nineteenth-century homileticians called a skeleton or a brief) to keep in mind the principal ideas
- Preparation of a complete manuscript without any attempt to repeat its language[13]

If all of these methods are extemporaneous, then we must conclude that its essence is the free utterance of words that are born in the moment of speaking them. Dabney gave the best definition: "I mean by it a discourse in which the thought has been perfectly prearranged, but the words, except in cardinal propositions, are left to the free suggestions of the moment."[14]

Broadus warned, "No intelligent man would now propose that preachers should habitually speak extempore, as regards the *matter*."[15] However, he warmly recommended extemporizing the language of the sermon and catalogued the advantages of extemporary address:

- It "accustoms one to think more rapidly."
- It frees up time for preachers to concentrate on preparing their thoughts.
- It also frees up time for self-improvement and pastoral work. (Dr. Mark Dever is one of the best full-manuscript preachers I know. He told me that he would have a whole extra day a week available if he did not write out his sermons. In contrast, another fine full-manuscript preacher, Dr. Robbie Crouse, told me that he saves time by writing because he is a particularly quick writer.)
- In the act of delivery, the preacher can take into account new insights, which are frequently the best of all.
- These new and superior thoughts lift the preacher's soul and the entire sermon.
- The preacher can read the audience and purposely alter expressions "according to his own feeling and that of the audience."

- The extemporaneous preacher is more apparently dependent upon the Holy Spirit in the act of preaching.
- Only extemporaneous speech "can ever be perfectly natural, and achieve the highest effect."
- Proficiency in extemporaneous speech opens up "many opportunities for usefulness."
- "With the masses of the people, it is the *popular* method."[16]

Although these advantages may seem to be unassailable arguments in favor of extemporaneous address, Broadus also listed some weighty disadvantages:

- "Perhaps the gravest of them all consists in the tendency to neglect of preparation, after one has gained facility in unaided thinking and extemporaneous expression."
- "There is a difficulty in fixing the mind upon the work of preparation without writing in full."
- It can "prevent one's forming the habit of writing."
- The sermon cannot so easily be used again.
- Extemporaneous preachers cannot quote extensively. (This seems a trivial objection, because they can have longer quotations in written form and shouldn't be quoting extensively in the first place!)
- "The *style* of an extemporaneous sermon is apt to be less condensed and less finished."
- "A similar and more serious disadvantage is the danger of making blunders in statement."
- "The success of an extemporaneous sermon is largely

dependent upon the preacher's feelings at the time of delivery, and upon the circumstances."
- "The reaction and nervous depression following extemporaneous preaching are apt to be greater than in the other cases."[17]

In Chapter 5, I will return to some of these disadvantages and try to discourage certain preachers from practicing extemporaneous delivery, including some who are most naturally inclined toward it. I have certainly experienced both the advantages and the disadvantages of extemporaneous preaching, as I related in the Introduction. I've preached a few sermons that left everyone (especially me) stunned. Many others have fallen flat, leading me to ask if anyone present, including myself, was alive. This is one of the thrilling risks of extemporaneous preaching—you never know what is going to happen. My friends who are among the best manuscript preachers are more consistent in their preaching than I am. I always know what to expect from them, and I always know that it will be good. I never fear that they will fail to preach a solid sermon. Their structure is excellent, their word choice superb, their illustrations and applications on target, and their treatment of the text worthy of publication. However, I don't generally anticipate that anything extraordinary will happen when they preach. They inevitably leave me edified, so the sermons are great successes, but they less often leave me deeply stirred.

Someone may reasonably conclude that we should prefer the method that tends to produce the most consistent results, which would be reading. In so doing, we would be more likely to avoid the worst sermons. However, at the same time, we would also reduce the probability of producing the occasional sublime ones.

You Make Me Want To Shout! (or Chat)

Before we proceed, it is important to clarify that I am talking about a method, not a style. Unfortunately, there are two styles sometimes identified with the extemporaneous method, one that is perennial and another that has become popular recently. The first is shouting. The second is chatting.

Regarding shouting, some preachers have given extemporaneous preaching a bad name by confusing eloquence and vehemence. Although I do not understand how, ranting orators are sometimes able to delude their audiences into thinking that they are actually saying something. I was once a judge for a high school speech contest in which one young man stole the show by raising his voice, gesticulating wildly, and finally jumping off the stage with his fist in the air. He electrified the audience, and the two other judges voted for him, not recognizing that his words had been "full of sound and fury, signifying nothing." For my part, I voted for the young woman who quietly and nervously delivered a well-organized speech with serious content of importance to her. I could not persuade the other judges, but I privately told the young woman that I appreciated her speech and considered it superior. She was understandably frustrated and said something to me along the lines of, "At least I said something!" No matter how bad our delivery during a given sermon, may we always be able to say, "At least I said something."

In his discussion of variety in sermon delivery, Dabney noted:

> There is a grave error to which energetic minds are very liable: it is that of attempting to be brilliant, emphatic or impas-

sioned throughout the whole discourse. No monotony is so dreary as that of the speech which is monotonously boisterous.[18]

The error of trying to emphasize everything is particularly common among young preachers, and it can be easily fixed but only if recognized as an error. Aristotle humorously described young men:

> All their mistakes are in the direction of doing things excessively and vehemently. They disobey Chilon's precept by overdoing everything; they love too much and hate too much, and the same thing with everything else. They think they know everything, and are always quite sure about it; this, in fact, is why they overdo everything.[19]

I sure did. Because my early preaching efforts were at a street corner, I developed an exuberant style necessary to capture and hold people's attention for a few minutes as they waited for a bus. After I had preached one of my early student sermons in a seminary classroom, Dr. John Bettler bluntly told me, "I'm glad you can hit the golf ball far. Now you need to learn to place it." In fact, he was pleased to have something with which to work. I too would rather have to teach students to channel excessive energy than have to try to light a fire under them. However, if they never learn to control their enthusiasm, they are going to become experts at first exciting and then wearying congregations.

As counterexamples to this caricature of extemporaneous preachers as uniformly boisterous, there have been powerful extemporaneous preachers who have maintained a calm demeanor throughout their sermons and their entire ministries. As a university student, I got to hear many wonderful speakers at conferences sponsored by InterVarsity Christian Fellowship. At one, Dr. Edmund Clowney spoke. He was a thin man, his voice cracked occasionally, and he tended to fall into a regular cadence in his sentences. Although his presence did not initially command my attention, somewhere along the way, he had me transfixed by his preaching of Christ from the list of David's mighty men. At the time, I had no idea how he had pulled that off, but I wanted to find out, so I eventually ended up as his student at Westminster Seminary and have tried to emulate his redemptive-historical approach to preaching ever since. The explanation of the power of Clowney's sermons is that biblical content is more important than delivery. Delivery is a means to the end of getting God's Word to people's minds and hearts and wills and must never exalt itself into being an end in itself. At least delivery should not get in the way of good content; at best it should magnify it.

The other extreme may be more common today, the tendency to give a casual and witty chat. Over the decades, preachers have imitated the style of prominent orators. Some evangelists became the Christian version of the smooth-talking salesman, adept at closing the deal. Some highly educated preachers borrowed from the academy, wanting to be known for their mastery of the language, their beautiful metaphors, their impressive vocabulary, their quotations of classical literature. Others donned business suits and power ties, imitating the competency of the managerial class and inspiring people with the superior brands of their churches. Today's casual preachers have reacted to the identification of the preacher with the salesman, professor, or CEO. However, they have unwittingly fallen into the same error, only with updated trappings. The model is still the eloquent orator as defined by the current generation, but now with hip cultural references, self-referential and often self-exalting humor, casual coolness, earthy language. The new patterns to imitate are the TED talker, the social media master, the late-night comedian, the motivational speaker, and the self-help guru. As a confirmation of this tendency, a friend of mine recently praised his formerly favorite, now disgraced, preacher by saying, "So-and-so was the best preacher I have ever heard! He was so funny!" My friend had no idea how damning was his praise.

John Piper identified the underlying similarities between two contrasting styles under the title of *professionalism*:

> Among younger pastors the talk is less about therapeutic and managerial professionalization and more about communication or contextualization. The language of "professionalization" is seldom used in these regards, but the quiet pressure felt by many pastors is: Be as good as the professional media folks, especially the cool anti-heroes and the most subtle comedians.
>
> This is not the overstated professionalism of the three-piece suit and the power offices of the upper floors, but the understated professionalism of torn blue jeans and the savvy inner ring. This professionalism is not learned in pursuing an MBA, but by being in the know about the ever-changing entertainment and media world.
>
> This is the professionalization of ambience, and tone, and idiom, and timing, and banter. It is more intuitive and less taught. More style and less technique. More feel and less force.

> If this can be called *professionalism*, what does it have in common with the older version? Everything that matters.[20]

I once attended the church of one of the most famous casual preachers, who has mastered the use of media technology and perfected his conversational and witty communication style. He has reputedly reached many people with the gospel. The sermon he preached that day was a very good treatment of a text about the lordship of Christ. However, in my opinion, his style undercut his effectiveness as he strolled around or propped himself on a barstool and made funny aside comments. His content called us to take Jesus seriously, but the style assured us that we could be relaxed about Christ's demands.

The best aspect of this casual style is that it is popular, not in the sense of being the most applauded but in the sense of being of the people. About this sort of popularity, Dabney wrote, "All public speakers should employ, as nearly as the dignity of the subjects will allow, the dialect of the people, and use their vocabulary."[21] Because the conversational preachers excel at this kind of popularity (of the people), they also tend to become popular in the common sense of the word (liked by many people). People like to listen to preachers who speak their language. However, if their style becomes too base for the sublime message that it purports to communicate, it undercuts itself. Also, because it is too tied to current communication trends, it will soon be outmoded, just like those of yesteryear that now seem to us so imitative.

With regard to current communication styles, we must use them if we want to connect with people. However, we need to keep in mind three caveats. First, they can be great servants, but they are terrible masters. That is, although we must use current styles, we must not make them absolutes or allow them to exercise unnatural control over us. (If a preacher develops unnatural habits early on, it is hard to break them later.) Second, while it goes too far to say that the "medium is the message,"[22] the medium is never neutral but always affects the message, enforcing it or undercutting it. For example, preachers who rage about God's tenderness or joke about God's justice undercut their message, while those who naturally get choked up over God's mercy and tremble as they speak of the Day of Judgment possess an almost irresistible eloquence. Third, trends in public speaking are ephemeral and will quickly pass away, so we must not be so attached to them that we cannot abandon them when they lose their effectiveness.

Does Method Matter?

Getting back to our three methods, and in the light of their respective benefits and pitfalls, one could reasonably conclude that all preachers have gifts and abilities that will incline them toward one method or the other or toward a prudent combination of all three. In fact, this is exactly what happens and inevitably so. Our talents, gifts, inclinations, experiences, training, and models all coalesce into a personal method of preaching that we adopt and practice. However, this fact does not mean that all three methods are equally good or that we automatically adopt the one that is best for us. Without disparaging any preacher or any effective method, I want to encourage more preachers to develop their extemporaneous abilities. Chapters 3 and 4 explain and recommend the method more amply, while Chapter 5 offers warnings about its common abuses. Chapter 6 relates what happens when preachers speak their sermons.

However, before we continue, we will consider in Chapter 2 why public speaking is so difficult in the first place.

---

1. James A. Broadus, *A Treatise on the Preparation and Delivery of Sermons*, Revised by Edwin Charles Dargan in 1898 (New York and London: Harper & Brothers Publishers, 1970), 439–41.
2. Broadus, 451.
3. Broadus, 451–2.
4. Robert Lewis Dabney, *Lectures on Sacred Rhetoric*, 1870 (Carlisle, PA: The Banner of Truth Trust, 1979), 331–32.
5. Alexander, *Thoughts on Preaching*, 1–2. During the civil war in the Roman Empire, Pompey and Julius Caesar battled for control. After suffering a defeat, Pompey sailed to Egypt, where he thought King Ptolemy would give him refuge. Instead, an officer of Ptolemy killed Pompey upon his arrival.
6. Marcus Tullius Cicero, trans. and ed. J. S. Watson, *On Oratory and Orators* (Carbondale: Southern Illinois UP, 1970), 176.
7. Broadus, 440.
8. Broadus, 441–46.
9. Dabney, *Sacred Rhetoric,* 328.
10. Broadus, 446.
11. James W. Alexander, *The Life of Archibald Alexander, D.D., LL. D., First Professor in the Theological Seminary at Princeton, New Jersey* (Philadelphia, 1870), 113.
12. See Dabney's *Sacred Rhetoric*, 339, Broadus, 465, and Alexander's *Thoughts on Preaching*, 160–61.
13. Broadus, 456–57.
14. Dabney*, Sacred Rhetoric*, 332.
15. Broadus, 457.
16. Broadus, 458–63.
17. Broadus, 464–69.
18. Dabney, *Sacred Rhetoric*, 320.
19. Aristotle, *Rhetoric*, in *Aristotle: II*, Vol. 9 of Great Books of the Western World, ed. Robert Maynard Hutchins (Chicago: Encyclopedia Britannica, Inc., 1952), 636; bk. 2, ch. 12.
20. John Piper, ed., *Still Not Professionals* (Minneapolis: Desiring God, 2013), 1–2.
21. Dabney, *Sacred Rhetoric*, 286.
22. Marshall McLuhan coined this phrase in his 1964 book, *Understanding Media: The Extensions of Man.*

Chapter 2
Why Public Speaking Is So Difficult

If humans are uniquely gifted for speech, and if most of us speak effortlessly and constantly, why is *public* speaking so difficult? Most people find speaking in public to be immeasurably more difficult than speaking to others in a private setting, and most of those who find it equally easy do it very badly.

Why do our palms perspire, hands shake, minds freeze up, voices crack, and our thoughts race or become jumbled? Why do we become so unnatural and employ unusual means to appear natural? Why do we so often misjudge our audiences and fail to connect with them? As far as I can tell, there are no definitive answers to these questions, so I offer some possibilities that may help us overcome some of the obstacles if only by being aware of them.

French Reformed preacher Adolphe Monod (1802–1856) wrote an article on "The Delivery of Sermons." He pointed out the basic difficulty of public speaking:

> It must be borne in mind, in the first place, that there is a wide distinction between preaching and conversation,

however grave, interesting, or animated. A discourse, in which it is attempted to develop one or more propositions, one person being sole speaker for an hour, before a numerous audience, has, and ought to have, something of continuity and elevation which does not belong to mere conversation. We are no longer in the sphere of simple nature. There must be some calculation of measures, management of voice, and strengthening of intonations; in a word, there must be *self-observation*; and where this begins, the speaker is no longer in that pure simplicity where nature displays and acts itself forth unreservedly. Preaching likewise demands certain powers, both physical and moral, which are not possessed by everyone, and which are not required in conversation. The two cases, therefore, are not parallel; and this may suffice to show how the same persons may succeed in one and fail in the other.[1]

To build on Monod's observations, we can observe first of all that public speaking is always in some sense unnatural because the situations are contrived. In normal human speech, we follow cultural conventions about when to speak, how long to speak, on what topics to speak in each setting, etc. When all conversation partners follow these unwritten rules, the discussion can be delightful and illuminating as it flows along unhindered. When one or more of the conversation partners breaks the prevailing conventions, the entire interaction is ruined. For example, sometimes there are overbearing participants who monopolize the conversation, effectively silencing the more reserved. If in such a situation a friend notices that John has not said anything and wants to bring him into the conversation (and perhaps shut up the loud-mouth), he may say, "John, you've been quiet. Would you like to say something?"

Although kind on the friend's part, the invitation makes John miserable, because any intervention he makes at that point will be forced, out-of-turn, unnatural, and contrived. John may have had brilliant comments to make along the way, but the conversation swept on, and his comments were no longer appropriate. He cannot smoothly bring them up later.

Public speaking settings are much like this awkward conversation, because they violate the unwritten rules of conversation. The rhetorical situation silences everyone except the appointed speaker to whom it turns and says, "Would you like to say something?" The speaker then needs to overcome the awkwardness of the contrived setting and bring the audience into as natural a state as possible. This observation is not to denigrate public meetings, lectures, sermons, or speeches. It is merely to observe that they are created situations that are, to one degree or another, unnatural.

Second, public speaking situations focus everyone on the speaker, causing him or her to be especially self-conscious. Why humans become more self-conscious when others are looking at us is a question I cannot answer, but most people confess it to be the case. For humans, this increased self-consciousness can produce positive results by forcing us to take others into account and adjust our words and actions accordingly.[2] However, self-consciousness can also be paralyzing or at least highly distorting. Monod observed, "But to declaim, to take a new tone, because one is in the pulpit—[that is], to speak as no one ever speaks, is a grievous fault; while, strange to say, it is a fault very common, very hard to avoid, and which, perhaps, none of us escapes altogether."[3]

Third, public speaking occasions provide no convenient cover or way of escape. In normal conversations, we can, if charitably inclined, help each other out and cover over a multitude of errors. However, in public speaking, there is no one to cover for us. If we fail, we do so alone and in the sight of all. It is not a team sport where the praise or blame falls on all the teammates. It is a solo high-wire act with no safety net, a fact that makes both speaker and audience nervous.

Fourth, public speaking is always, in some sense, a performance. No matter how humble the preacher and how spiritually-minded the audience, the fact that public speaking involves one person addressing many makes it subject to evaluation as a performance. The speaker and the hearers naturally and spontaneously raise scorecards in their own minds and in their subsequent conversations. As they take their evaluations out into the actual or virtual community, the speaker gains a reputation for eloquence, power, brilliance, humor, etc., or the lack of these.

Fifth, for pastors especially, there are many other concerns that intrude upon the act of preaching. There are a few churches that have a designated pastor of preaching who spends the entire time preparing and preaching, unconcerned with the mundane affairs of running the church or shepherding the people. While it is a questionable practice to divorce preaching from shepherding, it is also not an option that many churches can afford. Therefore, most pastors are concerned, like Martha, about many legitimate things: the spiritual and physical health of the congregation, elders and deacons, paid staff, volunteers, music, finances, buildings, outreach, attendance, missions, etc.

When responsible pastors stand up to preach, they grieve for the couple that suffered a miscarriage, the marriage that is on the rocks, the man who just lost his job, and the woman who just lost her husband. They notice the level of the attendance, the new person in the back whom no one has greeted, the song that no one knows how to sing, the piano that sounds out of tune, the leak in the ceiling, and the noisy fan. That they can teach a text of Scripture in any coherent way is nothing short of amazing with all of the legitimate concerns and distractions that pull in multiple directions.

By the way, my own recent experience confirms the destructive power of these concerns on one's preaching. After twenty years in our church in Guadalajara, Mexico, other people were covering most of the ministry areas, and the church was growing consistently with new believers. Although I sometimes preached three or four times on Sunday, preaching was my main concern, so I could remain focused. Also, there was such sympathy between the congregations and me that the preaching often seemed effortless.

After returning to the United States, we began working to start another new church from scratch, and my preaching suffered terribly as a result. I had a hard time figuring out why I was nervous, awkward, restrained, unnatural, tentative. In addition to my Sunday preaching, I also was teaching a weekly Bible study at a retirement village. A fellow pastor heard me at both venues and asked me why I was so much better (freer, more forceful, more humorous, more natural, etc.) at the retirement village than in my own church.

My immediate answer helped me understand what was happening. In my church, I was concerned about many things (including survival). But at the retirement village, I was concerned about one thing—doing the hearers spiritual good by teaching them God's Word. While Sundays still present many distractions for me as a solo church planter, I am trying to concentrate on doing only the one thing necessary while I am preaching, and the results have been positive.

The sixth and final reason for the difficulty of preaching in particular is because of the weightiness of the subject matter and its consequences. We preach God's Word, and the stakes are incalculably high—life or death for our hearers and for us. Impressed by the task of declaring the gospel, Paul wrote:

> *But thanks be to God, who in Christ always leads us in triumphal procession, and through us spreads the fragrance of the knowledge of him everywhere. For we are the aroma of Christ to God among those who are being saved and among those who are perishing, to one a fragrance from death to death, to the other a fragrance from life to life.*

No wonder he then asked, "*Who is sufficient for these things?*" (2 Cor. 2:14–16).

In light of all these complications and obstacles to effective public speaking and preaching, what is the way forward? Monod noted that "the power with which certain men speak, and the excellence of their delivery, arise in great measure from their ability to put themselves perfectly at their ease in a position where others are embarrassed."[4] Monod granted that some are more naturally confident than others, but the real key for the preacher lies elsewhere. He wrote:

> But there is another element which enters into this ease of manner, and I both wish it for you, and enjoin it upon you—it is *Faith*. Take your position as the ambassador of Jesus Christ, sent by God to treat with sinful men; believe that He who sends you will not leave you to speak in vain; labor for the salvation of those whom you address, as if it were your own; so forget yourself to see only the glory of God and the

salvation of your hearers; you will then tremble more before God, but less before men. You will then speak with liberty, therefore with the same facility and propriety which you possess in the other circumstances of life. If our faith were perfect, we should scarcely be in more danger of falling into false or declamatory tones, than if we were crying out to a drowning man to seize the rope which is thrown out to save him.[5]

Dabney emphasized the other side of the same coin: to preach by faith is to preach by God's grace, for we receive grace by faith. In his words, "If my readers rise from the perusal with these two convictions enhanced in their souls—that it is grace which makes the preacher, and that nothing is preaching which is not expository of the Scriptures—my work is not in vain."[6] In other words, the way for preachers to overcome the many obstacles to effective preaching is to be people of faith, trusting in God's grace alone, and to be expositors of Scripture alone.

Practically speaking, faith in God's grace manifests itself in prayer. J. C. Harrison reported about Monod's life and preaching, "His manner was singularly natural and unaffected, without the slightest appearance of self-consciousness."[7] According to Harrison, Monod attained this naturalness through prayerful piety and study:

Moreover, he was a very devout man. All the truths which he preached had first been as fuel to the devotion of his own heart. He had not only studied them, but by prayer had wrought them into the very structure of his own soul. They had been the life of his life, the very strength of his spirit; for he emphatically lived and walked with God. In unreserved conversation he had sometimes told me how the early hour of devotion (for he was an early riser) was the renewal of his life, how it braced him for the work of the day, how it projected its benign and sacred influence over his duties and pleasures. This early season of devotion he held sacred, and allowed nothing to intrude on or diminish it. Its effect was evident in his preaching, throughout which an air of devotion invariably ran, imparting to it not the mere warmth of animal spirits, or of brilliant imagination, but the glow of heaven itself.[8]

Although I hope to provide some practical help in speaking, nothing will contribute as much to the effective delivery of our sermons as the practice of personal devotion and piety in both life and ministry. Without these, any practical advice one might find here or elsewhere is useless or worse. Therefore, before we continue, let's pray:

A MINISTER'S PREACHING
MY MASTER GOD,
I am desired to preach today,
but go weak and needy to my task;
Yet I long that people might be edified with divine truth,
that an honest testimony might be borne for thee;
Give me assistance in preaching and prayer,
with heart uplifted for grace and unction.
Present to my view things pertinent to my subject,
with fullness of matter and clarity of thought,
proper expressions, fluency, fervency,
a feeling sense of the things I preach,
and grace to apply them to men's consciences.
Keep me conscious all the while of my defects,

and let me not gloat in pride over my performance.
Help me to offer a testimony for thyself,
and to leave sinners inexcusable in neglecting thy mercy.
Give me freedom to open the sorrows of thy people,
and to set before them comforting considerations.
Attend with power the truth preached,
and awaken the attention of my slothful audience.
May thy people be refreshed, melted, convicted,
comforted, and help me to use the strongest arguments
drawn from Christ's incarnation and sufferings,
that men might be made holy.
I myself need thy support, comfort, strength, holiness,
that I might be a pure channel of thy grace,
and be able to do something for thee;
Give me then refreshment among thy people,
and help me not to treat excellent matter in a defective
way, or bear a broken testimony to so worthy a redeemer,
or be harsh in treating of Christ's death, its design and
end, from lack of warmth and fervency.
And keep me in tune with thee as I do this work.[9]

---

1. Adolphe Monod, "The Delivery of Sermons," *Select Discourses by Adolphe Monod, Krummacher, Tholuck, and Julius Müeller* (New York: Sheldon, Blakeman & Company, 1858), 397.
2. There are, of course, some people who seem to have no awareness of the effects of their words and actions on others, but these people generally say and do things that are so inappropriate that they are not likely to be good public speakers, except perhaps as provocateurs who stir passions or buffoons who amuse people without themselves really understanding what is so funny.
3. Monod, 406.
4. Monod, 399.
5. Monod, 400.
6. Dabney, *Sacred Rhetoric*, 7.

7. J. C. Harrison, "Reminiscences of Adolphe Monod, the Great French Preacher," *The Evangelical Magazine and Missionary Chronicle* (March 1861), 145.
8. Harrison, 145.
9. Arthur Bennett, ed., *The Valley of Vision: A Collection of Puritan Prayers and Devotions* (Edinburgh: The Banner of Truth Trust, 1975), 191.

Chapter 3
A Little Help From My Friends

The first recorded example of extemporaneous speaking was when God said, "*Let there be light*" (Gen. 1:3). A most amazing thing happened after God spoke—there was light! A little later on, God spoke saying, "*Let us make man in our image, after our likeness*" (Gen. 1:26). Theologians have debated the question of what constitutes the image of God and have repeatedly lost their way by trying to find something *in* God or *in* humans that is his image. The idea is actually simpler and at the same time more expansive. Humans *are* the image of God. In other words, we humans are the creatures that most resemble God. Where some theologians go astray is by trying to limit the resemblance to one or a few characteristics instead of recognizing that we resemble God in many ways.

One of the most fascinating ways in which we reflect God is by speaking. Although investigators have made some surprising and fascinating discoveries about animal communication, even more startling and settled is the vast chasm between the most sophisticated animal communication and the simplest human speech.

God spoke and created things. We speak and create things as well, certainly not new physical matter but friendships and enmities, marriages and divorces, war declarations and peace accords, revolutions and reforms. We produce vibrations of air that flow from our mouths into others' ears, a purely physical phenomenon. Amazingly, we use and interpret these vibrations to create thoughts and feelings in others, and they are able to do the same in us. We accomplish so much of this creative activity by means of extemporaneous speech.

In this chapter I won't provide a history of extemporaneous speaking, since that would be impossible. I'll explore the *theory* of extemporaneous public speaking or oral delivery. I have the delight in this chapter of introducing you to some of my teachers, mentioning part of their general contributions to communication theory and then focusing in on each thinker's special contributions to the question of speech delivery. Although this may be understood, I am not endorsing *what* all these authors wrote or said on many topics but learning from *how* they spoke and taught others to speak.

Classical Rhetoric Made Simple

Three, three, three, three, five, six. Remember these numbers, and you have classical rhetoric in a nutshell:

- *three* means of persuasion
- *three* genres
- *three* aims
- *three* styles
- *five* canons
- *six* parts

Aristotle (384–322 BC)

The author of the first systematic treatment of rhetoric, Aristotle defined it as "the faculty of observing in any given case the available means of persuasion."[1] His connection of rhetoric to persuasion persists in most approaches to communication to this day. He also contributed the first two "threes," which also continue to appear in many public speaking books. The three means of persuasion are ethos, logos, and pathos. They are appeals based on the character of the speaker, on the content of the argument, and on the emotions of the hearers. The three genres of speech are the deliberative (for an assembly), the forensic (for the courts), and the epideictic (for ceremonies).

Although Aristotle did not devote a section of his *Rhetoric* to delivery, he was the first (to my knowledge) to record a fundamental observation about the basic difference between speaking and writing, one that is foundational to the recommendation of extemporaneous speech in preaching:

> The written style is more finished; the spoken admits of dramatic delivery…. Compared with those of others, the speeches of professional writers sound thin in actual contests. Those of the orators, on the other hand, are good to hear spoken, but look amateurish enough when they pass into the hands of a reader. This is just because they are so well suited for an actual tussle, and therefore contain many dramatic touches, which, being robbed of all dramatic rendering, fail to do their own proper work, and consequently look silly.[2]

In other words, speaking and writing are distinct verbal genres, each powerful in its place and weaker outside of it. In general, written speeches, when heard, lack punch. Spoken discourses, when later written down and read, lack polish.

Marcus Tullius Cicero (106–43 BC)

Cicero contributed or at least clarified the third and fourth "threes," the "five," and the "six." In his *Orator*, he identified the three aims of oratory and the corresponding three styles that accomplish those aims. They are:

- to prove, accomplished by the plain style,
- to please, accomplished by the middle style, and
- to persuade, accomplished by the grand style.[3]

He added that the most eloquent orator uses all three styles according to the overarching principle of propriety, or that which is appropriate:

> Now the man who controls and combines these three varied styles needs rare judgment and great endowment; for he will decide what is needed at any point, and will be able to speak in any way which the case requires. For after all the foundation of eloquence, as of everything else, is wisdom. In an oration, as in life, nothing is harder than to determine what is appropriate.[4]

In keeping with this goal of propriety, he warned against common errors in delivery. For example, the orator that overuses the grand style, especially without preparing the hearers, will sound like "a raving madman among the sane, like a drunken reveller [sic] in the midst of sober men."[5] He also warned against premeditated jokes but recommended spontaneous humor.[6] He further cautioned the orator on the one hand against rambling and on the other against "cementing his words together too smoothly," since there is "something agreeable" about "a not unpleasant carelessness on the part of a man who is paying more attention to thought than to words."[7] His constant conviction was that proper training and extensive writing would prepare orators to find the best words at any moment to express their thoughts.[8]

Cicero clearly listed the five canons in his *De Inventione* (*The Treatise on Rhetorical Invention*). He acknowledged that "numerous writers have laid them down."[9] In Latin, these canons are *inventio, dispositio, elocutio, memoria,* and *pronuntiatio* or *actio.* The English equivalents (invention, arrangement, style, memory, and delivery) often appear in eighteenth- and nineteenth-century homiletics works.

Once identified, the canons are rather obvious. First, speakers need to invent what they are going to say. Second, they need to arrange them in a form that flows logically. Third, they must develop a pleasing style of presentation that will help their audience hear and understand their ideas. Fourth, they must find a way to store necessary aspects of the speech in their memories for easy retrieval during the speech. Fifth, they stand and deliver the speech to the audience.

He also delineated the six constituent parts of a speech:

> And these portions appear to us to be in all six; the exordium, the relation of the fact, the division of the different circumstances and topics, the bringing forward of evidence, the finding fault with the action which has been done, and the peroration.[10]

These are otherwise known as introduction, statement of facts, division, proof, refutation, and conclusion. These divisions are appropriate for the kind of forensic or deliberative speech that Cicero most often practiced, and they affected generations of speakers and preachers, forcing an artificial template onto every speech.

Perhaps every generation has its favorite templates, and it is common for some preachers to structure every sermon in the same way, regardless of the flow of the text. One common template these days is: 1) The text tells you to do this. 2) You can't do it. 3) Christ did it, so trust him. The use of this or any other fixed outline flattens out the beautiful and variegated contours of Scripture.

At the very end of the third and final book of his *De Oratore* (*On Oratory*), through the mouth of Crassus, Cicero exalted delivery as of paramount importance, calling it the canon "that has the sole and supreme power in oratory."[11] He also made anecdotal comments about the use of the voice, eyes, and the body. However, he recommended no particular method of delivery, probably because he linked delivery to nature more than to art. Crassus did mention the exercise of reading Greek orators and translating them into Latin on the fly, which forced him spontaneously to find the most appropriate words in his native tongue to express the thoughts, which is precisely what extemporaneous speech does.[12]

Also, Cicero's historical context often demanded that delivery be extemporaneous. He lived in the dying days of the Roman Republic during which urgent public speaking was of the utmost importance as the future of the Republic hung in the balance. Many of the references to speeches in *De Oratore* were from the Roman forum or courts in which read or memorized speeches would have generally been impossible except in the opening arguments.

In *Orator,* he sought to describe the Platonic ideal orator, one that he admitted never existed, although he seemed to think that he came close! Along the way, he gave helpful speaking tips, examples, and exercises and concluded with a simple summary: "As a matter of fact, the art of delivering a beautiful oration in an effective oratorical style is nothing else… than presenting the best thoughts in the choicest language."[13]

Marcus Fabius Quintilian (c. 35–100)

No rhetorician followed Cicero more closely than did Marcus Fabius Quintilian. However, in place of Cicero's bantering conversations, Quintilian offered a systematic program for the formation of orators all the way from cradle to career. Although not credited with original genius, it is fair to call Quintilian the great systematizer of classical rhetoric. Following Demosthenes and Cicero, Quintilian considered delivery "the most potent factor of all in oratory."[14] Regarding the relationship between writing and speaking, Quintilian supposed that they are distinct activities and stressed that they support each other:

> Certainly, writing is never more necessary than when we have to improvise a lot.[15] It is the way in which weightiness can be maintained, and the superficial verbal facility acquires some depth…. It may well be that if we do both these things with care and persistence, each will help the other: we shall speak more accurately because we write, and write more fluently because we speak.[16]

Also, Quintilian recommended something very close to sermon notes:

> Pleaders who are often in court commonly write out the essentials, at least the introductory parts, cover the rest of what they do at home by mental preparation, and meet sudden contingencies by improvising.[17] Cicero's notebooks show that this is what he did.[18]

He added, "In this connection, I certainly allow such brief notes and books as can be held in the hand and which we may legitimately glance at from time to time."[19] Although he certainly did not invent the use of lecture or sermon notes, we may credit Quintilian with the first clear instructions on how to use them effectively.

In addition to these instructions, Quintilian also has the distinction of being the first to explicitly discuss the relative benefits of two delivery methods: reciting and extemporizing. He did not seem to contemplate the possibility that someone might actually read a speech. He wrote, "This diversity of natural ability has given rise to a doubt whether, before making a speech, one should learn it by heart word for word, or whether it is enough simply to grasp the essentials of the facts and their order. Of course, no universal rule can be laid down."[20] However, Quintilian expressed his preference for verbatim memorization, because it avoided the choppiness caused by looking at notes, because it took best advantage of the benefits of writing, and because it gave the impression of great intelligence if the speaker could deliver it *as if extemporizing*, in essence by faking spontaneity, even pausing as if searching for the right words.[21] This last idea seems to be a backhanded admission that extemporizing is better, since the reciter is most effective when trying to give the impression of speaking words born in the moment.

François Fénelon (1651–1715)

Not trying to be exhaustive but including the authors I find most instructive, I jump ahead more than a millennium to French Roman Catholic priest, François Fénelon, whose *Dialogues on Eloquence* treated the subject of sermon delivery methods explicitly in his bantering dialogues among imaginary interlocutors.

Following Cicero, Fénelon conceived of rhetoric as unperceived art that imitates nature. In praising Demosthenes, Fénelon wrote, "It is nature herself who speaks in this ecstasy—the art is so perfect that it does not appear anywhere—nothing ever equaled his rapidity and vehemence."[22] Again, "everything the speaker does ought to follow nature," and "The sight of a large audience and the importance of the subject which he is handling ought surely to stir a man much more than if he were engaged in an ordinary conversation. But in public as in private he must always act naturally."[23]

Because of his emphasis on natural delivery, Fénelon rejected the recitation of memorized sermons, which was the common practice in his day among Roman Catholics in France. He wrote:

> The entire art of the good orator consists only in observing what nature does when she is not hampered. Do not do what bad speakers do in striving always to declaim and never talk to their listeners. On the contrary, each one of your listeners

must suppose that you are speaking particularly to him. There you have what produces natural, familiar, and suggestive tones.[24]

And he continued:

On the other hand, I assume the well-informed man who is filled with his subject and has great facility in speaking… in short, the man who thinks deeply upon all the principles of the subject that he must handle and upon all their ramifications, who puts them in order in his mind, who devises the strongest utterances to make his subject visible, who arranges all his arguments, who prepares a certain number of striking figures. This man unquestionably knows everything that he must say and the place where he must put each thing. The only thing that remains for him to do is to find ordinary diction to give the necessary body to the speech.[25]

Fénelon went on to assume that his ideal orator would be "well practiced in writing, as Cicero requires."[26] Further, he granted that Demosthenes and Cicero wrote out their speeches, but he also insisted that they did not memorize them. He seems to have assumed that the extemporizer would depend on no written material in the act of delivery:

On the contrary, he [Cicero] appears to limit himself to the wish that the speaker arrange carefully all parts of his speech in his mind and prearrange figures and central terms to be used, reserving to himself the opportunity to throw in on the spur of the moment whatever necessity and the design of things would inspire. It is out of such considerations, indeed, that he demands so much diligence and presence of mind on the part of the orator.[27]

One of the alleged inferiorities of extemporaneous address, noted by Broadus, is its tendency toward errors of grammar, diction, or pronunciation, which Fénelon excused and even celebrated:

> His sentences will not delight the ear so much. All the better. He will be a better orator for that. His transitions will not be so subtle. That doesn't matter. Besides his being able to have prepared them without getting them by rote, he will have the additional advantage of sharing such negligence with the most eloquent orators of antiquity, who believed that they must often copy nature in this respect and not show too complete a preparation.... At the most, you will find in his speech some inexact construction, some term that is improper or that has been condemned by the Academy, some element of irregularity or if you wish something weak and badly placed, which would have slipped out in the heat of battle. But one would have to have a small mind to hold these to be great errors. One will find some of them in the greatest classics. The most skillful of the ancients ignored them. If we had horizons as wide as theirs, we would scarcely be preoccupied with these trifles.[28]

In other words, because of the small errors inherent in extemporaneous address, the hearers will inescapably know that a human being is *speaking* to them and be delighted by the experience.

George Campbell (1719–1796)

Scottish Presbyterian George Campbell was one of the most cited rhetoricians of the eighteenth century. Campbell's *Lectures on Systematic Theology and Pulpit Eloquence* was required reading when Dabney was a student at Union Theological Seminary and was still the basic textbook at Union when Dabney first arrived as professor. In the preface to his *Lectures on Sacred Rhetoric*, Dabney named Campbell's *Philosophy of Rhetoric* in his list of seven "exceedingly instructive" sources, while he included *Lectures on Pulpit Eloquence* in the list of works also included in his studies.[29]

Campbell addressed the subject of delivery but discussed only two possibilities:

> The consideration of these things hath often led me to doubt, which of the two methods of delivery, reading or repeating [reciting], we ought to recommend to students, or at least which of the two, if universal, would probably have the best effect, and be attended with the fewest disadvantages.[30]

He first recognized what he considered an indisputable fact: "That a discourse well spoken hath a stronger effect than one well read, will hardly bear a question."[31] This fact led Campbell early in his career to prefer reciting to reading. However, a sobering fact caused him to revise his early conclusion. Not many preachers were gifted speakers, and art could not create what nature had not endowed. Therefore, he admitted the possibility of reading sermons as the best available option to the less fluent.

Actually, after his meek concession, Campbell inserted a

parenthetical lament about the fact that the education of his day did not adequately prepare young men to learn to be good speakers.[32] Frankly, his few pages on sermon delivery did little to improve the situation. However, he almost stumbled on a solution when he observed:

> I have known ministers whose sing-song manner in preaching was a perfect soporific to the audience, pronounce their speeches in the General Assembly [of the Church of Scotland] with great propriety and energy. The only account I can make of this difference is, that in the two former cases, in the senate and at the bar, the speeches are almost always spoken. Committing the whole, word for word, to memory, is, I believe, very rarely attempted. Now the General Assembly partakes of the nature of both a senate and court of judicature. Sermons, on the contrary, are more generally repeated. They are few who trust to a talent of speaking extempore in the pulpit. Now when once the attention, as was hinted already, loses hold of the thought, and is wholly occupied in tracing the series of words, the speaker insensibly, to relieve himself from the difficulty of keeping up his voice at the same stretch, falls into a kind of tune, which, without any regard to the sense of what is said, returns as regularly, as if it were played on an instrument.[33]

The surprising conclusion of this keen observation (which really repeats Aristotle's) was to argue in favor of reading instead of reciting. The logical conclusion would have been to argue for speaking rather than reading *or* reciting. However, it appears that Campbell's context, in which few attempted extemporaneous preaching, kept him from arriving at the logical conclusion of his own arguments and observations. It fell rather to Richard Whately to develop the implications of Campbell's observations.

Richard Whately (1787–1863)

Bishop Richard Whately of the Church of England first published his *Elements of Rhetoric* in 1828, and it appeared in several successive editions over the next two decades. In terms of his basic views of rhetoric, like the other Enlightenment rhetoricians, he defined it as a practical art designed to perfect nature.[34] Whately shared the Enlightenment optimism about the operation of universal rules or laws. The art of rhetoric discovered its universal rules by observing the practice of good speakers and systematizing the principles they practiced. He advocated what he called the "free, natural, and simple style."[35] He helpfully gave specific instructions about how to develop such a style:

> And the substance of what is to be spoken on each occasion should be, after reflection, written down; not in the words designed to be uttered (for that would, instead of a help toward the habit of framing expressions extempore, prove an embarrassment), but in brief heads, forming such an outline as in the preceding section has been recommended; that as little as possible be left for the speaker to frame at the moment except the mere expressions. By degrees, when practice shall have produced greater self-possession and readiness, a less and less full outline previously written down will suffice; and in time the habit will be generated of occasionally forming correct judgments, and sound and well-expressed arguments, on the spur of the moment.[36]

By the way, Whately's recommendation of incremental movement toward greater extemporaneity is what I have experienced in my preaching ministry. After my early efforts with a complete manuscript before me, over the years, I have followed what has been a natural process of reducing the number of pages I take into the pulpit. At one point, I reduced the number to zero, but then I bounced back up to two or three since I found that it took longer to prepare when I used no notes than when I used two pages, and going paper-free afforded little advantage during my delivery.

Speaking of paper-free, let me mention the use of electronic devices. While I appreciate and use modern technology in many ways, I have found that preaching from a device lends itself best to reading since the screen allows one to see only a section of the sermon rather than scan its whole flow at a glance. In the early days of electronic tablets, a friend who films and edits for television told me that news anchors did not like them, because paper better enabled them to see the context of what they were presenting. I once used an electronic tablet in a wedding ceremony where there was much reading of set formulae, but I cannot preach freely from one (and decided not to use it in weddings anymore either). Also, I have discovered that the one who lives by electronics dies by them too. Batteries run down, screens go blank, drives freeze up, and Internet connections falter. In many other contexts, my devices are handy, but in the pulpit, I want only a large-print Bible and very few typed pages of outline.

Of greatest interest for our present purposes is Whately's fourth part where he carefully analyzed the differences between reading and speaking, which he considered one of his novel contributions to rhetorical theory. Indeed, while Aristotle noted the difference, and Campbell almost stumbled on it, Whately truly did break ground in his analysis. He stated that the purpose of public reading is to place the hearer in the same position as the reader, to place the text before the hearer, to communicate to the hearers "thus and thus is written in the book or manuscript before me."[37] Through the oral medium, reading thrusts the text before the audience. In contrast, speaking, or what Whately called "natural speaking," "conveys, by the sounds which reach the ear, the idea, that what is said is the immediate effusion of the Speaker's own mind, which he is desirous of imparting to others."[38]

As a decisive proof of the difference between reading and speaking, Whately offered the example of someone overhearing another's voice from a nearby room without being able to make out the sense of the words being uttered. Whately plausibly claimed that the hearer "will hardly ever be for a moment at a loss to decide whether he is *Reading* or *Speaking*."[39] We can repeat this experiment easily with so many audio sermon recordings available online. Perhaps without being able to say exactly how we know, we will have little trouble determining if the preacher is reading or speaking freely. In a footnote on the same page, Whately cited Thomas Sheridan's repeated experiment of placing a book in the hand of an animated speaker, asking him to read it and observing the complete transformation of his delivery. As quoted by Whately, Sheridan concluded, "A different pitch of voice took place of his natural one, and a tedious uniformity of cadence succeeded to a spirited variety; insomuch that a blind man could hardly conceive the person who read to be the same who had just been speaking."[40]

From this analysis, Whately proceeded to distinguish between two methods of teaching good extemporaneous delivery, pejoratively named the Artificial and the Natural. As the primary example of the artificial method, he condemned the Elocutionist systems, which tried to discover and establish rules of utterance to which the speaker must learn to conform.[41] It would be anachronistic in our day to attack the Elocutionists, but we have something equivalent in our pulpits. I know men who are animated and delightful conversationalists around a table among friends, but when they ascend to the pulpit, they try to "sound like a preacher," probably imitating, consciously or unconsciously, the preaching they have heard. The effect is disconcerting and ineffective, precisely because it is so unnatural. Not only do these men not usually speak in such a forced manner, but no human being does.

Whately's simple counterproposal to teaching rules of eloquence was that the speaker should focus entirely on content and let delivery take care of itself:

> That nature, or custom, which is a second nature, suggests spontaneously these different modes of giving expression to the different thoughts, feelings, and designs, which are present to the mind of any one who, without study, is speaking in earnest his own sentiments. Then, if this be the case, why not leave nature to do her own work? Impress the mind fully with the sentiments, &c. to be uttered; withdraw the attention from the sound, and fix it on the sense; and nature, or habit, will spontaneously suggest the proper delivery.[42]

Whately regarded this forgetfulness of self as not only rhetorically but also morally excellent.[43]

He anticipated some of the supposed drawbacks of extemporaneous delivery that Broadus catalogued. For example, extemporaneous speech is naturally more faulty and repetitive than written language, but charmingly so.[44] With regard to the nervousness of the extemporaneous preacher, Whately noted its salutary effect on the hearers, as they are "perceiving themselves to be personally *addressed*, and feeling that he is not merely reciting something *before* them, but saying it *to* them. The speaker and the hearers will thus be brought into a new and closer relation to each other."[45] Thus did Whately approach what Dabney would later call the communion of souls, which was also essential in Monod's and Spurgeon's homiletics.

I could include others with profit in this historical and theoretical review of extemporaneous delivery, including Ebenezer Porter (1772–1834) of Andover Seminary, French Abbot Louis Bautain (1796–1867), and Swiss Protestant Theologian Alexandre Vinet (1797–1847). However, I leave those as recommendations for further study and move on to some princes of the nineteenth-century pulpit, the Alexanders, Spurgeon, and Dabney, having already quoted rather extensively from Broadus.

Archibald Alexander (1772–1851)

A native Virginian, Archibald Alexander spent much of his adult life in the North, first as pastor of Pine Street Presbyterian Church in Philadelphia and then as the first Professor of Didactic and Polemical Theology of the newly formed Princeton Seminary, where he also taught Pastoral Theology and Homiletics.[46] He formed his practice of preaching as a young man during a time of revival in the hinterlands of Virginia. James Alexander recorded words from his father's memoirs:

> The thing [public "exhortation"] was new in that part of the country, and many came together. I was exceedingly apprehensive that I should utterly fail, and not be able to say anything, for I had never spoken in public except what I had committed to memory.[47]

The young man who preceded Alexander did in fact fail utterly. His turn arriving, Alexander reported what happened:

> After another prayer and hymn, I was called upon. Although I did not know a single word which I was to utter, I began with a rapidity and fluency equal to any I have enjoyed to this day. I was astonished at myself, and as I was young and small, the old people were not less astonished. From this time, I exhorted at one place and another, several times every week.[48]

I have already related his defining experience at the church where his notes blew away. His son concluded:

> [T]hroughout his life, the extemporaneous discourses of Dr. Alexander, which indeed were the highest effusions of his mind, partook of the character of these early efforts; and he has been heard to say again and again, that if he were to stake his life on a single effort, he would, if familiar with the general subject, abandon himself entirely to the impulse of the moment.[49]

At Princeton Seminary, Alexander taught to students what he himself practiced. He generally discouraged the reading of sermons, which was the almost universal practice in the North among educated ministers. This posture brought him into open disagreement with his younger colleague, Charles Hodge, who responded to a General Assembly "resolution against reading sermons in the pulpit" by advocating reading as evidence of a mature church.[50] Alexander found no such connection between ecclesiastical maturity and sermon reading, continued to promote extemporaneous preaching, and feared that written sermons would induce a preacher to forget "that lively sense of his dependence on Divine aid which the preacher ought to feel."[51]

James W. Alexander (1804–1859)

Born in Virginia, James Alexander also spent much of his life in the North. He pastored churches in New York and, for a brief period, taught as Professor of Rhetoric and Belles Lettres at the College of New Jersey. Today, he may be recognized as the translator of the hymn "O Sacred Head Now Wounded." An admirer and emulator of his father, James Alexander's unsystematic and posthumous work, *Thoughts on Preaching*, reflects lessons learned from the elder Alexander. In fact, his first thought was:

> Formalism of sermons.—Without flattering myself with the notion that I was ever eloquent, I am persuaded that the most effective discourses I ever delivered, were those for which I had made the least regular preparation. I wish I could make sermons as if I had never heard or read how they are made by other people. The formalism of regular divisions and applications is deadly. And as to written sermons, what is written with weariness is heard with weariness.[52]

In one of the thoughts in which he referred to his own

preaching entitled "Offhand writing," Alexander lamented, "And why have I, contrary to my natural turn, always preached in the commonplace humdrum manner, instead of giving free vent to the things that come into my head?"[53] In another thought, he confessed, "I sometimes think I never acted out my inner man in a sermon. The nearest approach had been extempore."[54] As practical advice to attain the rhetorical heights of extempore address, he wrote, "In delivery, learn to know when to dwell on a point; let the enlargement be, not where you *determined* in your closet it should be; but where you feel the spring flowing as you speak *let it gush*. Let contemplation have place *while you speak*."[55] He summarized his own approach: "The principle from which I set out, is one which grows in my esteem every day, as a canon of composition: it is this—*In writing or speaking throw off all restraint.*"[56]

The second part of Alexander's work consists of ten letters written to young ministers on various subjects related to preaching. He intended to write only one letter on extempore preaching, which he also called "free utterance," but it stretched to three. He refused to condemn outright the reading of sermons, rejected preaching impromptu as to the content, and defended extemporaneous preaching.[57] He insisted, "Digest the subject, but be not careful to choose your *words* previous to your delivery."[58] Again, "But if you would avail yourself of the plastic power of excitement in a great assembly to create for the gushing thought a mould of fitting diction, you will not spend a moment on the words."[59]

More radical and perhaps terrifying in his recommendation to young ministers than Whately (who advocated small steps toward freer utterance), Alexander gave this advice and challenge:

If you press me to say which is absolutely the best practice in regard to "notes," properly so called, that is in distinction from a complete manuscript, I unhesitatingly say, USE NONE. Carry no scrap of writing into the pulpit. Let your scheme, with all its branches, be written on your mental tablet. The practice will be invaluable. I know a public speaker about my age, who has never employed a note of any kind. But while this is a counsel for which, if you follow it you will thank me as long as you live, I am pretty sure you have not courage and self-denial to make the venture.[60]

My own advice and experience are closer to Whately's, but perhaps I lacked the courage and self-denial to try my hand at paperless preaching earlier in my life.

Charles Haddon Spurgeon (1834–1892)

The least systematic, most famous, and most entertaining of the nineteenth-century homileticians was Charles Spurgeon of London's Metropolitan Tabernacle. Thousands flocked to hear him preach each week. Millions more have read his printed sermons that were transcribed and edited from his extemporaneous addresses. I have always been amazed at Spurgeon's multiple accomplishments, including an orphanage, a pastor's college, a huge building project, and the oversight of multiple societies. One of the reasons he was able to accomplish so much was that he generally prepared his Sunday morning sermon on Saturday night and took a half sheet of notes with him into the pulpit. He was able to spend so little time on specific preparation because he read voraciously and was thus constantly preparing.

He strongly discouraged both reading and what I have called impromptu preaching:

> Here let me say, *if you would be listened to, do not extemporise in the emphatic sense*, for that is as bad as reading, or perhaps worse, unless the manuscript was written extemporaneously; I mean without previous study. Do not go into the pulpit and say the first thing that comes to hand, for the uppermost thing with most men is mere froth. Your people need discourses which have been prayed over and laboriously prepared. People do not want raw food; it must be cooked and made ready for them. We must give out of our very souls, in the words which naturally suggest themselves, the matter which has been as thoroughly prepared by us as it possibly could have been by a sermon-writer; indeed, it should be even better prepared, if we would speak well. The best method is, in my judgment, that in which the man does not extemporise the matter, but extemporizes the words; the language comes to him at the moment, the theme has been well thought out, and like a master in Israel he speaks of that which he knows, and testifies to what he has seen.[61]

Spurgeon added little to homiletical theory except his amusing aphorisms. He agreed with others that writing was beneficial, that impromptu preaching was necessary on occasion but not the best regular method, and that extempore speech was generally superior to recitation or reading.[62] He provided plenty of useful tips for preachers. Following his own practice, he observed, "If a man would speak without any present study, he must usually study much."[63] The two tools that he recommended for developing extemporaneous speech were an abundant "store of ideas" and a "rich vocabulary."⁶⁴ In order to master the tool of speech, Spurgeon recommended learning another language.⁶⁵

At this point, let me give a plug for missionary service, especially among a people who speak a different language than your mother tongue. While this must not be the primary motivation for becoming a missionary, I have personally found language study to be one of the best mental exercises available since it forces the brain to juggle concepts, competing vocabularies, phonemes, syntaxes, and local expressions to find the best way to express a matter.

Since our church in Guadalajara had an English-speaking congregation and a Spanish-speaking one, I preached in each language to separate congregations. For a while, I prepared two sets of sermon notes, but I dropped the practice and began to use my Spanish notes to preach both sermons. Especially in the English service, this practice forced me to go for the ideas and find the right words to express them in the moment. Yes, this method sometimes tripped me up, as when a word in the other language would slip out inadvertently, but this generally proved to be a source of delight to the congregation, as the people intuitively sensed that a man was earnestly speaking to them with some of the normal foibles of human speech in a bilingual setting.

With reference to these verbal slips, which I am liable to make in English and in Spanish, Spurgeon offered an excellent piece of advice: "Let me whisper—for it is meant for your ears alone—it is always a bad thing to go back. If you make a verbal blunder, go on, and do not notice it."⁶⁶ By the way, as you read Spurgeon's polished printed sermons, do not be too intimidated, for his verbal errors were edited out.

Spurgeon warned that extemporaneous ability is difficult to achieve but easy to lose, telling of his own experience of a creeping dependence on external helps in preaching if he allowed them. He wrote, "If for two successive Sundays I make my notes a little longer and fuller than usual, I find on the third occasion that I require them longer still."[67] I discovered the same in my return to the United States to start a new church. Preaching in my church in Guadalajara was generally a delight because I felt so comfortable there. Also, I was the only pastor many in the church had ever known, so they did not compare me to others.

Starting over in Florida with new people, many of whom had been at different times in churches with popular preachers, I tried to get my sermons just right. I prepared earlier in the week and composed my notes with great precision. However, for most of a year, the results were the opposite of what I had hoped for. The magic of Mexico was gone, and I became tied to my notes, constrained, tentative, self-aware, uncertain, and needlessly complicated. Only through prayer and great effort have I begun to recover some of my former extemporaneous ability. I have had to force myself to throw off my self-imposed constraints.

Spurgeon provided comfort in this sort of situation, reminding us:

> It may save you much surprise and grief if you are forewarned that there will be great variations in your power of utterance. To-day your tongue may be the pen of a ready writer, to-morrow your thought and words may be alike frost-bound.[68]

His warning was not "to become sufficient as of yourself," remembering, "if the Lord should leave you you will be at a dead stand." His advice? "Your variable moods of fluency and difficulty will by God's grace tend to keep you humbly looking up to the strong for strength."[69] In this regard, I thank God for my difficult struggles in preaching after returning to the United States, because they reminded me again of my utter dependence on God.

Robert Lewis Dabney (1820–98)

Robert Lewis Dabney, Virginia native and graduate of Hampden-Sydney College, the University of Virginia, and the Southern Presbyterian Church's Union Theological Seminary, later became professor at Union, first of Ecclesiastical History and Polity and later of Systematic and Polemic Theology. Before assuming his professorship, he served one year as an itinerant Presbyterian missionary to his home county of Louisa and for six years as pastor of Tinkling Spring Presbyterian Church. During most of his years at the Seminary, he also worked as co-pastor at the College Church. He served briefly as a chaplain in the Confederate Army and later as chief of staff to General Thomas "Stonewall" Jackson.

After the war, he grew embittered and worked on fruitless plans to transport the Old South to a foreign country. Eventually poor health and changing sentiments at Union Seminary led him to leave his beloved Virginia and assume the chair of Moral Philosophy as one of the original professors of the new University of Texas, located in the more hospitable climate of Austin. Although he continued teaching and preaching after becoming completely blind in 1890, the University of Texas eventually edged the conservative and orthodox Dabney out of his professorship.

As a young man training for the ministry, Dabney, like

Archibald Alexander, had a defining experience that shaped his preaching. After the first sermon he preached in a church, he wrote to his mother:

> I am convinced by my first trial that I can never read sermons to my people in any comfort. *Extempore* preaching is the thing for me. I could notice the difference plainly between the paragraphs I threw in, although not expressed with half as much propriety of language as that which was on paper. It is much more important that sinners should be excited to listen to truth than that I should have the reputation of a pretty writer.[70]

He developed his extemporaneous ability during his itinerant ministry and at his settled pastorate. By the time he returned to the seminary as a professor, he was already recognized as a powerful preacher. Finding no suitable textbook to teach students, he published his own *Lectures on Sacred Rhetoric*, which made a strong impression on me during my first pastorate.

Although a simplification, it is possible to derive many if not all of Dabney's ideas from two basic concepts—the preacher as a herald of God's Word and preaching as the communion of souls. For Dabney, the idea of preachers as heralds of God's Word meant that they should stick as closely to the biblical text as possible. Although this idea is simple, it was pregnant with implications in Dabney's mind, requiring some practices and forbidding others. For example, it required in the preacher wide learning, deep knowledge of the Bible, careful exegesis, ability to instruct, scrupulous personal piety, consistent emphasis on Christ, confidence in the Bible's own testimony, and charity even toward opponents. At the same time, the idea of preachers as heralds ruled out secular or political subjects, a reliance on philosophy, excessive argumentation or polemics, insincerity, self-promotion or ostentation, unbridled humor, and sarcasm or ridicule.

Significantly for our present purpose, this idea also demands extemporaneous ability for two reasons. First, according to Dabney, extemporaneous delivery is the most natural and therefore the most sincere. As the most sincere form of delivery, it is also the most fitting for one whose job it is to announce the holy will of the King. Second, the herald's job requires the ability to explain orally God's will found in the written text of the Bible.

Dabney's second basic principle was his elevated concept of preaching as communion between the soul of the preacher and the souls of the hearers. To be fair, the idea of soul-to-soul communication in preaching was not Dabney's invention. Others (Bautain and Monod) had emphasized it earlier than Dabney, as did his contemporary, Spurgeon. For example, Monod wrote, "I cannot then, repeat too often, speak *ex animo* (*out of the soul*). Perhaps you think this is a matter of course, and that the advice is unimportant. But practice will convince you that it is not so."[71]

Even so, Dabney was the one who made most clearly the argument that this concept of preaching requires extemporaneous delivery. In order to connect with their hearers, in order to impress their souls upon the audience, in order to commune with them, preachers must look at them and speak to them, reporting not merely the words they composed in private but the ideas arising at that very moment, spontaneously expressed in language born in the act of delivery. According to Dabney, the read or recited sermon places a written barrier between the preacher and the congregation, while the extemporized sermon brings the two into direct contact. Therefore, only extempore preaching rises to the level of preaching as communion of souls.

With regard to the classical canon of invention, Dabney did not permit preachers as heralds to invent their matter, which is the Scripture alone. However, he followed Swiss Protestant theologian Alexandre Vinet in extending invention to cover delivery.[72] Dabney added, "The method, the style, the diction, the gesticulation, all must be invented."[73] In criticizing the reading of sermon manuscripts, Dabney observed, "Even if the matter and style are rhetorical, the action cannot be, but it is almost impossible that the structure either of thought or language should be such, when the invention is performed in solitude and at the writing-desk."[74] In contrast, he found the great benefit of extemporary preaching to be the need to invent the sermon as it is preached:

> The capital advantage is that the mind is required to perform over again the labour of invention, during the actual delivery of the discourse. It is thus aroused and nerved. The condition of its success is, that it must again represent to itself in a living form the whole thought and emotion of the discourse; that it must, in a word, recreate it in the act of delivering it. It is only such a discourse, actually born in its delivery (if it is a second birth), a living progeny of the soul, that has true movement.[75]

Some say that those who do not write out full manuscripts are not putting enough effort into their sermon preparation. For example, in the anthology on sermon preparation that I mentioned in the Introduction, one contributor went so far as to reprimand all preachers who do not write out a full sermon manuscript, telling us to sit down.[76] The idea is that we who do not write out full manuscripts are stopping the process short so that it does not come to full fruition. We are leaving blanks to be filled in, perhaps carelessly, later. Admittedly, this is a common fault of extemporaneous preachers and one to try to avoid by careful preparation, usually including writing. However, I have the same concern about writing complete manuscripts, that the sermon production process is truncated. Once the words are written down, the invention stops before the people get a thrilling taste of it.

As I have already stated and now repeat, I personally know some excellent manuscript preachers. Although I cannot get inside their heads to know what mental processes are occurring during the preaching, I am guessing that the best of these really are inventing in the moment. As far as I can tell, they are not exactly reading their manuscripts. They have written everything out, have gone over it multiple times, and have fixed the whole flow in their minds so that a quick glance at their manuscript serves the same purpose as my quick glance at my outline—to provide a reminder sufficient to carry them through that whole section of the sermon. The words they speak may be virtually the same as the ones they wrote, but not because the preachers are merely retrieving them from the page and depositing them on the congregation but because they were the best words during the writing phase and occur to the preacher anew as the best words during the delivery. These preachers do, in fact, invent them freshly as they preach. Dabney actually described and commended such a practice:

> For this purpose, they go over their sermon eight, twelve or even twenty times, until their recollection of the order of

thought is indelible, and until the whole soul is possessed and fired with the subject. They then take their manuscript into the pulpit and open it before them. The knowledge that they can recur to it at every moment sets them at ease from the fear of losing the thread or hesitating for words. The whole train of thought and the face of the manuscript are so fixed in the memory, that few and rapid glances enable them to give almost the very words of the writing; but they do not make any conscious effort to adhere to, or depart from those words. They feel that they can do the former in any instant, for the words are before them, and they were selected with care, for their appropriateness; but if an impulse possesses them to modify the language of any passage, it is also easy to do this. They select with facility either of these alternatives which the awakened and impassioned mind prefers at the moment; and in many places, where nearly the exact language of the manuscript is, in fact, retained, yet the utterance really has the quality of *extempore* eloquence, because there is a process of invention at the time.[77]

Dabney and other extemporaneous homileticians sometimes sounded dogmatic in principle, but they were flexible in practice and allowed for differing gifts and proclivities. However, he was inflexible on this point: invention must extend to the delivery of the sermon in order for it to be alive enough for the soul of the preacher to commune with the souls of the hearers.

This chapter covered outstanding rhetoricians and preachers on the theory of extemporaneous speaking. In the next, we move on to learning its practice.

———————————

1. Aristotle, 595; bk. 1, ch. 2.
2. Aristotle, 666; bk. 2, ch. 12.
3. Marcus Tullius Cicero, *Cicero V: Brutus, Orator*, trans. H.M. Hubbell (Cambridge, MA: Harvard UP, 1962), 357; ch. 21, par. 69–70.
4. Cicero, *Brutus, Orator*, 357; ch. 21, par. 7
5. Cicero, *Brutus, Orator*, 379; ch. 28, par. 99.
6. Cicero, *Brutus, Orator*, 371; ch. 26, par. 89.
7. Cicero, *Brutus, Orator*, 363; ch. 23, par. 77.
8. Cicero, *Brutus, Orator*, 475; ch. 58, par. 200.
9. Marcus Tullius Cicero, tr. C. D. Yonge, *The Treatise on Rhetorical Invention*. (Digireads.com Publishing, 2010), bk. 1, ch. 7.
10. Cicero, *Rhetorical Invention*, bk. 1, ch. 14.
11. Cicero, *On Oratory and Orators*, 255; bk. 3, ch. 56.
12. Cicero, *On Oratory and Orators*, 43–44; bk. 1, ch. 34.
13. Cicero, *Brutus, Orator*, 499; ch. 67, par. 227.
14. Marcus Fabius Quintilian, *The Orator's Education*, trans. Donald A. Russell (Cambridge, MA: Harvard UP, 2001), 4:261; bk. 10, ch. 1, par. 17.
15. The inelegant phrase "when we have to improvise a lot" translates "*cuando cum multa dicemus ex tempore.*"
16. Quintilian, 4:385–87; bk. 10, ch. 7, par. 28–29.
17. The phrase "meet sudden contingencies by improvising" translates "*subitis ex tempore occurrant.*"
18. Quintilian, 4:387; bk. 10, ch. 7, par. 30.
19. Quintilian, 4:387–89; bk. 10, ch. 7, par. 31–32.
20. Quintilian, 5:81; bk. 11, ch. 2, par. 44.
21. Quintilian, 5:81–83; bk. 11, ch. 2, par. 44–48.
22. François Fénelon, trans. Wilbur Samuel Howell, *Dialogues on Eloquence*, ca. 1679 (Princeton: Princeton UP, 1951), 63.
23. Fénelon, 100.
24. Fénelon, 104.
25. Fénelon, 106.
26. Fénelon, 107.
27. Fénelon, 110.
28. Fénelon, 107–08.
29. Dabney, *Sacred Rhetoric*, 5–6.
30. George Campbell, *Lectures on Systematic Theology and Pulpit Eloquence* (London, 1824), 219.
31. Campbell, 219
32. Campbell, 224.
33. Campbell, 223.
34. Richard Whately, *Elements of Rhetoric: Comprising an Analysis of the Laws of Moral Evidence and of Persuasion, with Rules for Argumentative Composition and Elocution*, 1848 (Carbondale: Southern Illinois UP, 1963), xxxiv.

35. Whately, 17, 23.
36. Whately, 32–33.
37. Whately, 341.
38. Whately, 342.
39. Whately, 342.
40. Whately, 342.
41. Whately, 344.
42. Whately, 350.
43. Whately, 367.
44. Whatley, 360.
45. Whately, 368–69.
46. The two sources for the material on Archibald Alexander are James W. Alexander's *The Life of Archibald Alexander, D.D., LL. D., First Professor in the Theological Seminary at Princeton, New Jersey* (Philadelphia, 1870), and James M. Garretson's *Princeton and Preaching: Archibald Alexander and the Christian Ministry* (Carlisle: The Banner of Truth Trust, 2005).
47. Alexander, *Life of Archibald Alexander*, 85
48. Alexander, *Life of Archibald Alexander*, 86.
49. Alexander, *Life of Archibald Alexander*, 86–87.
50. Garretson, 88.
51. Garretson, 93.
52. Alexander, *Thoughts on Preaching*, 1.
53. Alexander, *Thoughts on Preaching*, 5.
54. Alexander, *Thoughts on Preaching*, 19.
55. Alexander, *Thoughts on Preaching*, 18.
56. Alexander, *Thoughts on Preaching*, 20.
57. Alexander, *Thoughts on Preaching*, 147–49.
58. Alexander, *Thoughts on Preaching*, 151.
59. Alexander, *Thoughts on Preaching*, 152.
60. Alexander, *Thoughts on Preaching*, 151.
61. Spurgeon, Charles Haddon, *Lectures to My Students*, ca.1893 (Grand Rapids: Ministry Resources Library, 1954), 132.
62. Spurgeon, 140–42.
63. Spurgeon, 145.
64. Spurgeon, 146.
65. Spurgeon, 148.
66. Spurgeon, 150.
67. Spurgeon, 152.
68. Spurgeon, 152
69. Spurgeon, 152.
70. Thomas C. Johnson, *The Life and Letters of Robert Lewis Dabney*, 1903 (Carlisle: The Banner of Truth Trust, 1977), 87.
71. Monod, 405.

72. Alexandre Vinet, trans. Thomas H. Skinner, *Homiletics; or The Theory of Preaching* (NY, 1854), 3.
73. Dabney, *Sacred Rhetoric,* 50.
74. Dabney, *Sacred Rhetoric,* 328.
75. Dabney, *Sacred Rhetoric,* 333.
76. Douglas Sean O'Donnell, "Spirit-filled *Sitzfleisch*: The Prayerful Art of Sermonizing," in Rhett Dodson, ed., *Unashamed Workmen,* 212.
77. Dabney, *Sacred Rhetoric,* 330.

Chapter 4
How To Learn to Speak Well

In the anthology on sermon preparation that I mentioned in the Introduction, I arrived at what became my favorite chapter. The author was going through his steps and came to sermon delivery, where he wrote, "Not much to say about this,"[1] beside which I scribbled, "WHAT?" At first I was deflated. Maybe what fascinates me is of no interest to anyone else. Maybe I am stating only the obvious.

Then I was encouraged. Maybe no one is writing about sermon delivery, which is why someone should at least make the attempt. Also, the ancients agree with most people I know in placing delivery at the top of what makes a speech good. According to a story reported by Cicero in his *De Oratore*, Demosthenes considered delivery the first, second, and third most important aspects of eloquence. Cicero's Crassus commented, "Delivery, I say, has the sole and supreme power in oratory; without it, a speaker of the highest mental capacity can be held in no esteem; while one of moderate abilities, with this qualification, may surpass even those of the highest talent."[2] The power of delivery makes it exceedingly important for preaching, as well as a potentially dangerous trap.

Not the Main Thing

On vacation, our family attended the same church three times. We heard two preachers speak on consecutive Sundays and on the very same text. One spoke a mostly extemporaneous sermon with decent content. Another clutched the lower corners of the pulpit (reminding me of Joab in the Tabernacle waiting to be murdered) and read his complete manuscript, sometimes losing his place, stopping completely as he tried to find it, and repeating the same lines. He was hard to hear and understand. He did, however, deal carefully with the text at hand.

Some members of my family later admitted to checking out almost completely, and I cannot say that I blamed them. As a preacher, I try to give other preachers my undivided attention, and in this case, it took a supreme effort. As we were talking after the service, my family was surprised to find me preferring the sermon of the poor reader to that of the decent speaker. I thought his treatment of the text was much better. I realized once again the necessity, power, and danger of good speaking. It elevated the first sermon (masking its average content), and its absence nearly annihilated the second one (obscuring its better content). I do not think that my family is unique, since comments I hear about good and bad sermons likewise have much to do with *how* they are delivered. Perhaps there is a need to say something about delivery after all.

Even so, contra Demosthenes, delivery is not the most important aspect of preaching. Biblical content is. Sometimes

God kindly reminds me that my eloquence or lack thereof is not the main thing in preaching. One of my sermons that had the most visible effect surprised everyone, especially me since I had a severe case of laryngitis and could only croak hoarsely and with painful difficulty into the microphone. The text was one of Jesus' calls to follow him, and he called us that day. The congregation sat motionless and in absolute silence, stunned by the radical nature of discipleship, each one considering how to respond.

On other occasions I knew that the sermon was doing something to me and to the hearers because I could scarcely contain my emotions, and members in the congregation wept openly or shouted out in surprise or relief or joy. These manifestations were noteworthy in our context, first, because I am not given to public displays of emotion, and second, because our church did not express itself with such exuberance as a matter of course as some churches do.

The best measure of God's work in people through preaching is change in their lives and ours, which is often slow and cumulative and thus difficult to observe and quantify. Good preaching helps produce disciples over a period of years, but sometimes there are sudden breakthroughs.

A Christian man had convinced his wife to accompany him to our church along with their three children. We had been getting to know them and tried to minister to them during a health crisis. On Easter Sunday, I was preaching on Ecclesiastes 1 and 2. My sermon in the English service did not go well because I was more effective at driving home the vanity of life than I was in showing how the resurrection of Christ makes our lives and efforts *"not in vain"* (1 Cor. 15:58).

Feeling glum between the services, I asked another minister, Steve Hohenberger, some ten years older than I, for help with the sermon. He gently gave me one brilliant insight about the text that I had missed, and I incorporated that gem into the sermon in the Spanish service. The experience for the congregation and for me was entirely different, and especially for the woman who was starting to attend. It became plain to all that the resurrection of Christ completely overcame the futility of life under the sun. The woman wept uncontrollably, and we later discovered that her tears were the outward manifestation of God's regenerating work in her life. A few months later, after adequate preparation, we received the whole family into our church membership.

Normally, at least in my experience and that of my friends, the effects of preaching appear gradually as people begin believing the Gospel without necessarily knowing when they began to believe, when new believers' destructive habits start fading away, or when godly habits become more and more evident. Preachers often receive nice but possibly perfunctory compliments after the worship service. Much more gratifying are comments that come years later, when someone says:

> Do you remember when you said such and such in your sermon? Well, I was going through a very difficult time in my life when I knew that I needed to make a hard decision that was going to determine the direction of my future. Your sermon was the tipping point that enabled me to make that decision well. Thank, you pastor!

Also, we pastors have the gratifying experience of hearing conversations among members of our churches as they talk of wonderful things they have learned from God's Word, although they cannot recall how or where they learned them. We would ruin the conversation and rob ourselves of our reward if we reminded them that we preached on those things six times in the last thirteen years. Better to admire their learning and say in our hearts, "Thanks be to God."

We Can Do Better

Returning to the main theme of this book, how do we get better at speaking? As already mentioned, I received little instruction in this area in seminary, and rhetoric has mostly disappeared from university curriculums. It seems that only classical Christian schools care much about it.

Perhaps a first question we should ask is whether or not it is possible to improve at speaking. We must recognize that public speaking ability is a gift of nature and/or of the Holy Spirit. However, what do we have that is not a gift? (1 Cor. 4:7).

Also, gifts are distributed unevenly. Some persons are strong and graceful, while others are weak and clumsy. Some can sing like angels, while others growl off key. Some soar through school, while others barely pass each year. Some build bridges, while others can scarcely change a light bulb. However, almost all humans can speak spontaneously. If most of us can do it, then all of us can do it better.

In the United States, theological seminaries began in the early nineteenth century, when classical education was still the norm among those who were privileged to be educated. Seminaries could assume a certain mastery of grammar, logic, and rhetoric, other liberal arts, and classical languages. Their students had read some of the best authors, had received some tutoring in speaking, and had sat under classically educated older pastors, part of whose job was to train candidates for the ministry.

The situation is different today—in some ways better, in other ways worse. It is probably better for the church that more people aspire to be pastors who come from other vocations, having gained much useful world experience in trades and professions. However, it is also true that we enter ministerial training without much instruction or help in how to speak in public. How can we catch up before we step into pulpits? This chapter contains some suggestions about how to recover some of the advantages that our forebears enjoyed as a matter of course. It closes with specific ideas for a homiletics program that could be suggestive for a seminary, Bible college, or church setting.

Natural Ability

Cicero's Crassus mentioned three areas that are necessary to be a good orator: "natural capacity, moderate learning, and constant practice."[3] Expanding on these three requirements, he concluded:

> If the speaker or writer has but been liberally instructed in the learning proper for youth, and has an ardent attachment to study, and is assisted by natural endowments, and exercised in those indefinite questions on general subjects, and has chosen, at the same time, the most elegant writers and speakers to study and imitate, he will never, be assured, need instruction from such preceptors how to compose or embellish his language; so readily, in an abundance of matter, will nature herself, if she be but stimulated, fall without any guide into all the art of adorning eloquence.[4]

In terms of the natural capacities requisite for orators, he named first of all "lively powers in the mind and understanding, which may be acute to invent, fertile to explain and adorn, and strong and retentive to remember." In addition, he added "volubility of tongue, tone of voice, strength of lungs, and a peculiar conformation and aspect of the whole countenance and body."[5] While these are gifts of nature or of grace, which cannot be acquired, all admit that they can be developed. Crassus added encouragingly, "I am not ignorant that what is good may be made better by education, and what is not very good may be in some degree polished and amended."[6]

Dabney addressed the question of the possibility of learning public speaking in his "What is a Call to the Ministry?" As an encouragement to young men, he wrote:

> No young man whose vocal organs are not fatally maimed is entitled to conclude, because he is now unskilled, that he cannot learn to speak to edification. On the contrary, he should conclude that he *can learn* to speak, no matter what his difficulty, if only he will endeavor and persevere.[7]

One of the five classical canons of rhetoric is memory, which refers not only to the ability to recall but the techniques used to encourage retention and recall. Admittedly, a better memory will make extemporaneous delivery easier. However, there is hope for those whose memory is not the sharpest and for those whose memory is fading with age. I am beginning to find myself in the latter category since I'm around the age of sixty. For the first thirty years of my ministry, I found that words came to me with little effort, and I could sort among them, choosing the best ones as I spoke. Details from the biblical text or from history or theology or science or another field stuck with me and were available for spontaneous use at any time. Lately, I have found myself looking for the proper word, sometimes for what seems to me an awkwardly long time, and some details of Scripture have faded. To my horror, I have even made incorrect statements about details of Scripture, such as, for example, the chronological order of events in Old Testament history.

One potentially good solution for a weaker memory is to use more written material, something I have tried. However, in my case, depending more on my notes was counterproductive. It made me more awkward and hesitant, less connected to the congregation, and sometimes more confused as I had to search for words on the page instead of in my head.

Another solution is simply to know the material better by reviewing it more. In the past, I could write my notes, review them once or twice, and have them before me in my head on Sunday morning. Now I need to go over them again and again throughout the week, improving them each time. In addition to reading over them, I also can review them in my mind at idle times of the day, such as when I am trying to fall asleep.

Even as we work to mitigate the ill effects of aging on our preaching, we should recognize that aging brings benefits for preachers and hearers (that is, if we continue to be faithful in study and prayer and pastoral labor). If we diminish in youthful strength, range, or clarity of voice, or memory, or vigor of action, we can grow in exegetical ability and pastoral wisdom. This fact hit me when I was in my forties and invited an older man (who was then about my current age) to preach in my church one Sunday. His delivery was unremarkable, but I immediately recognized that his insight into Scripture and his ability to apply it to people were superior to mine. Hearing him made me look forward to the future when I could exchange fading winsomeness for increasing wisdom.

With regard to abilities for ministry, we need to remember one of Dabney's two cardinal points: it is grace that makes the preacher.[8] Paul, painfully aware of his disqualifications for ministry, understood that he was a preacher *by* God's grace in order to be a preacher *of* God's grace when he wrote:

> *Of this gospel I was made a minister according to the gift of God's grace, which was given me by the working of his power. To me, though I am the very least of all the saints, this grace was given, to preach to the Gentiles the unsearchable riches of Christ.* (Eph. 3:7–8)

This same Paul also said, *"But by the grace of God I am what I am, and his grace toward me was not in vain. On the contrary, I worked harder than any of them, though it was not I, but the grace of God that is with me"* (1 Cor. 15:10). In other words, God's grace toward us as preachers is not so that we might rest in mediocrity but rather work hard to improve upon the gifts he has given us. If we are contemplating our call to the ministry or are already in the ministry, how then may we all work to improve? Leaving aside natural capacity, we consider practical steps that are under our control: learning and practice. We begin with learning.

Read Good Books

In the United States, many universities use standardized tests to evaluate their applicants. These have sections that test mathematical and verbal aptitudes. Some now include writing sections, which at present are often ignored because of the subjectivity inherent in grading them. When I took the test in high school, I ended up with a mathematics score more than a third higher than my verbal score. I spent my university years studying mathematics and economics and trying to avoid courses that would require me to read or write much because I had concluded that verbal was not my area of strength. My first year, I struggled through what was called "Freshman Comp," a basic required writing composition course. By my final year, I had to write some long papers and met with passable success. Seminary was all about reading and writing and some speaking, and my confidence grew as my papers came back with good marks.

After entering the ministry, I realized that my basic Western Civilization and liberal arts education was still very deficient. Even after university and seminary, I still did not have the "general education" that Cicero's Crassus required. I had inherited a set of *Great Books of the Western World* and began, over a period of many years, to read some of them—Homer, Plato, Aristotle, Epictetus, Marcus Aurelius, Virgil, Augustine, Dante, Pascal, Locke, Swift, Rousseau, Mill, Melville, Tolstoy.

I listened to some as audiobooks and bought a series of university lectures on the Western intellectual tradition to try to fill in large gaps. I also alternated between reading dead authors and living ones (or at least more recently deceased ones). I have never read as widely or as quickly or as voraciously as some of my friends and colleagues, but slowly I managed to cover valuable territory. My family helped me as well since we educated our daughters at home and used a literature-based program. My wife and daughters would rave about books that I must read. My daughters continued the favor as they went off to university and sent home more recommendations.

During the appropriate years to have a mid-life crisis, I satisfied some of my restlessness by starting a doctorate in communication some sixteen years after I had graduated from seminary and at one of the busiest times of my life. The reading and writing load was several times what the seminary's had been, but I found that it was a pleasure, which surprised me since I began the program intimidated by some of my classmates, many of whom were already communication instructors or professors at the university level.

I concluded that a major help was my extensive reading over the years. Warning against young men ascending to the pulpit before they had much to say, Fénelon recommended, "A young man ought from time to time to test himself; but the study of good books should long continue to be his principal occupation."[9] Although Fénelon's advice may be ideal, it is also generally unrealistic, so it's better to consider the reading of good books to be lifelong continuing education.

The definition of "good books" will vary from person to person according to tastes and interests. However, any definition should include proper and elevated use of the mother tongue (either originally or in translation) and organized structure, not only of the overall argument but also of each chapter, paragraph, and sentence. I am not focusing so much on the content of the books but on their use of language. Good writers *master* language seemingly without effort. They are artists that do not draw attention to their artfulness.

This continuing education spills over not only into our writing but also into our speech. The goal is not to speak or write like Shakespeare or Milton or Hemingway. Rather, it is to learn how to use language well. Your vocabulary will grow, you will pick up new cadences, images will abound, and literary devices will start to become second nature. If things go well, you will not sound like any of these great authors. You will sound like you, tutored by all of them.

Write Often

Along with reading good books, we need to write often. Following Cicero and others, Dabney recommended, "One safeguard against this abuse of the *extempore* method is the constant use of the pen. Every minister must write much, whether he carries anything in the pulpit or not."[10] He insisted further:

> The abundant and painstaking use of the pen is necessary to give you correctness, perspicuity and elegance of language, and to make these easy to you. No man ever learns to compose a sermon at his desk in rhetorical language save by speaking *extempore* under the rhetorical impulse; so no man ever learns to speak well *extempore* save by learning to write well.[11]

Today everyone is a writer, at least on social media. For example, people routinely labor over short sentences to create maximum impact, hoping that they will garner attention from online friends and followers. At the same time, the emphasis on one-liners may be shriveling our ability to follow and develop a train of thought. It is more difficult to craft a good paragraph than a good sentence, a good chapter than a good paragraph, and a good book than a good chapter. To master social media, we need to become experts at one-liners and short articles. However, to develop our preaching, we need to write at length, but not verbosely, to sustain a long argument in the same direction.

The power of extensive and careful writing to elevate our thinking and speaking is the best argument in favor of writing out complete sermon manuscripts. Much better than the few pages of sermon notes that I compose, complete manuscripts can reveal and allow for correction of weaknesses before the Lord's Day arrives. I admit that I sometimes discover as I am preaching that the order of the thoughts in my notes is confused or confusing, and I am not always able to fix it on the spot. More extensive writing could help me to avoid such confusion. For this reason, some preachers recommend writing a full manuscript and then reducing it to a much shorter outline for use during the sermon. This adds to sermon preparation time, but it also could take advantage of the best of both worlds. Even Spurgeon recommended the writing of sermons, not in order to use a full manuscript in the pulpit, but to discipline the mind:

> Very strongly do I warn all of you against reading your sermons, but I recommend, as a most helpful exercise, and as a great aid toward attaining extemporising power, the frequent writing of them…. Leave them at home afterwards, but still write them out, that you may be preserved from a slipshod style.[12]

In addition to social media and sermon manuscripts or outlines, a preacher can keep a personal journal, write a blog, correspond with people around the world, send aptly written words of encouragement to church members, write courses, and submit articles and book manuscripts for possible publication. None of these efforts may win much acclaim, but they are valuable, since the goal is the development of true eloquence, not the inflation of the number of followers.

Listen to Good Speakers

I am guessing that many will immediately assume that I am promoting listening to recorded sermons by some of today's most admired preachers, and indeed it can be very beneficial to hear them. However, I do not have them particularly in mind when I recommend listening to good speakers. In fact, there can be a danger in listening to one or a few favorite preachers frequently, since we can consciously or unconsciously infer that the way they preach is how it should be done. If they are excellent expositors, we should indeed imitate their treatment of the text. However, imitating their style will not serve our congregations or ourselves well, and it will stunt our own development. When preachers imitate a famous preacher's style, the effect is generally disturbing for two reasons. First, they are not as good as the master. Second, they are not as good as they would be if they were not imitating someone else.

My recommendation is to listen to recorded masters of the language and to those naturally good speakers in our own contexts. I regret that we cannot hear Demosthenes or Cicero or Peter or Augustine or Spurgeon speak. Fénelon had to content himself with reading transcripts, observing, "The reading of good and bad orators will form your taste more surely than all the rules."[13]

To our advantage, we have access to audio recordings dating back into the second half of the nineteenth century and clear recordings from the earliest years of the twentieth century. Before the wide accessibility of high speed Internet, I ordered cassettes of sermons by D. Martyn Lloyd-Jones and John Murray and later purchased sets of cassettes or compact discs with collections of speeches—an anthology of great twentieth-century speeches,[14] a collection of Winston Churchill's most famous speeches, another of Ronald Reagan. I listened to these repeatedly and tried to interest my family in them as we rode in the car.

Especially during a moving Churchill speech, I would coach my young daughters, saying things like, "Did you hear what he just did there?" or "Listen to what's coming up. It's masterful!" or "Did you notice that pause? Wasn't it amazing?" At the time, they may have been merely amused at my exuberance, but they have turned out to be perceptive rhetorical critics in their own right, able to analyze speech and the techniques used therein. They also are becoming good public speakers. When our younger daughter would visit us back in Mexico while she was studying in the United States, she would help out with the music in the worship services and had to hear me preach three times, once in English and twice in Spanish. She admits that she listened to the sermon for herself one time and then maintained her interest in the other two services by noticing how I varied rhetorical strategies and techniques for each congregation.

My anthology of twentieth-century speeches includes many speakers to whom we do not normally listen, including United States presidents and military officers, British prime ministers and royals, baseball stars Babe Ruth and Hank Aaron, astronauts, Martin Luther King, Jr., Jesse Jackson, pilots Charles Lindbergh and Amelia Earhart, Malcolm X, and Gloria Steinem, among others. In addition to being of historical interest, these speeches give us good and sometimes bad examples of speaking. Also, by listening to many examples, there is less temptation to imitate the style of a favorite preacher. The effect is cumulative, learning to speak by hearing others do it well.

Not only can we listen to the masters of the past, but we can also search for the best speakers of the present. Where will we find them? Both Dabney and Bautain recommended paying attention to women and children, since they tend to be good natural speakers. Dabney recommended, "The public speaker should then study the gestures of natural feeling by observing the port of children, of gifted and animated women in social converse, and of true orators."[15]

Not naturally graceful, Dabney made a point of spending time in the company of refined women during his years at Hampden-Sydney College in order to improve the way he carried himself. Bautain claimed that women and children have advantages over men because they "speak willingly and with great ease, on account of their more impressionable sensibility, the delicacy of their organs, and their extreme mobility."[16]

Bautain meant these descriptions as high compliments, factors that contribute to what he called "expansiveness of heart." He flatly declared, "Women naturally speak better than men."[17] "Men, then, who wish to acquire the art of speaking, must learn by study[ing] what most women do naturally."[18]

In our family, we still recall some of our young daughters' spontaneous speeches as they held forth with passion about something that moved them deeply. I also vividly remember meetings in which the power of women's oratory was overwhelming. During a congregational meeting in our church, a topic came up that touched a woman in our church deeply and caught her completely off guard. She rose and gave one of the most passionate, orderly, and persuasive speeches I have heard in such an assembly. Otherwise, this same woman tends to shrink from public speaking other than in small women's groups.

In another setting, I had gotten tricked into participating in a seminar on the roles of women in the church. On the second day, after things had gone smoothly, a man showed up and rudely tried to stir up controversy, appointing himself the champion of oppressed women. However, the women themselves were uninterested in his valiant efforts to defend them. I tried to keep the peace, but the hero of the afternoon was a young woman of about twenty years who arose and gave an impassioned plea to the church at large that left me spellbound. I was one of the invited speakers, but that young woman gave me a lesson in oratory that day.

In addition to recorded speeches, women, and children, who else can teach us good oratory? This question is harder to answer than it should be, bombarded as we are by communication media. Radio and television talk shows are often examples of bombast and abuse, not eloquence. Of the many politicians in the world, only a few are gifted speakers, and we often have trouble getting past their political persuasions. There have been movies that contain eloquent speeches, but their effect is diminished by our knowledge that they were delivered by actors reciting their lines. Sometimes televised debates exhibit effective speech, but too often the debaters talk past each other or merely stick to their scripts and try to score points with quick jabs at their opponents.

Perhaps we need to return to what is most natural to us—listening to recorded sermons—since there is no organization so dedicated to and practiced in regular public speaking as the Christian church. However, in addition to the caveat I mentioned about not imitating the style of our favorite preachers, I offer a warning about another danger. We may overlook the content of a speech for the purpose of learning oratory. However, if we ignore the content of preaching with the goal of developing eloquence, we are in danger of not paying attention to God's proclaimed Word. A common trap for preachers and homiletics teachers is to become sermon critics instead of hearers and doers of the Word.

One Christmas Eve, on an occasion when several of us siblings were together at my parents' house, we attended a worship service and then gathered for dinner. Commenting on the sermon, someone at the table asked why the preacher tended to run out of breath at the end of his sentences. I observed that he over-aspirated his consonants, especially his sibilants, which used up his breath prematurely. My brother looked at me with admiration and pity, remarking about what an affliction it must be to notice such things in sermons. He was right.

For this reason, I find it better to listen to sermons in order to be instructed in God's Word and other types of oratory to study eloquence, even though I also inevitably learn eloquence from gifted preachers as an added benefit. When we teach homiletics, we have no choice but to critique the sermons of our students. Even so, we must also be willing to hear God's Word from them and from anyone else who faithfully proclaims it. Dr. Robbie Crouse and I currently share the responsibility of grading student sermons. He knows it is a good sermon when he stops grading and simply listens.

Remedial Education

If you are a younger preacher wanting to improve or an experienced preacher training candidates, how will you do it? In

Mexico, I was hampered by the lack of resources in Spanish, but English-speakers have an abundance of them. There are many excellent contemporary books on preaching. Because these are probably already familiar to readers, I would like to recommend some classics and others that built on the wisdom of the classics, which have helped me to understand the activity of preaching more deeply than more recent works. However, before we move on to rhetoric, it is necessary to mention the first two parts of the medieval trivium—grammar and logic.

Grammar

I remember diagramming sentences in ninth grade with Mrs. Roche, but somehow the grammar did not stick very well. Perhaps a late grammatical bloomer, I really began to grasp English grammar when I started studying Greek as an undergraduate. The painstaking tasks of memorizing and translating forced me to understand how the parts of speech work.

My understanding of English and Greek grammars took another leap forward when I studied Spanish, which heavily uses the subjunctive mood as Greek does. Not only did I have to read the subjunctive, but I also had to compose it in my own speech and writing. It is nearly impossible to pray in Spanish without it, whereas an infinitive will do nicely in English.

I mention my experience simply to illustrate that we cannot assume that graduates of secondary school, university, or even seminary are masters of grammar, so they may need to do remedial work as I did. Since I came at it late and through other languages, I do not have a particular English grammar textbook to recommend, but Mrs. Roche might, and many candidates would do well to purchase and study one.

If a grammar textbook is too remedial, and the preacher simply needs refining, a grammarian church member can be of great help. Spurgeon had an anonymous one in his congregation. He reported:

> When I was preaching at Surrey Gardens, an unknown censor of great ability used to send me a weekly list of mispronunciations and other slips of speech. He never signed his name, and that was my only cause of complaint against him, for he left me in a debt which I could not acknowledge.... Concerning some of these corrections, he was in error himself, but for the most part he was right, and his remarks enabled me to perceive and avoid many mistakes. I looked for his weekly memoranda with much interest, and I trust I am all the better for them.[19]

I had two or three in my Spanish-speaking congregation who did me a similar service. With characteristic Mexican kindness and tempered with effusive praise and apologies for bothering to mention anything, they gave me invaluable tips about mispronunciations, misused words, awkward constructions, or words that would have better expressed what they knew I was trying to say. I learned much from those brief conversations and was, like Spurgeon, the better for them.

Logic

As an undergraduate, I studied mathematics and economics. I was preparing for a career in business, but God redirected my path. As already mentioned, when I got to seminary, I was deficient in many areas of the humanities and significantly behind some of my contemporaries. However, one area in which I surpassed them was logic, which was helpful in seminary. It helped in exegesis, systematic theology, Hebrew, Greek, history, and apologetics. It has also helped in sermon composition since a built-in mechanism demands that my arguments flow logically from the text. In Chapter 5, I am going to recommend installing alarms into our heads, and here I mention the Non Sequitur Alarm, which clangs in my head when a conclusion does not follow from the premises. The way to install this crucial alarm is to study logic.

For undergraduate elective courses, I chose to take logic in the mathematics department and again in the philosophy department. In addition to these two courses, all my mathematics courses were themselves relentlessly logical. In my doctoral program, we read logic for the Philosophy and Communication course. The textbook was Irving Copi and Carl Cohen's *Introduction to Logic*, which I thought was excellent. However, there are others that are more geared toward working with syllogisms expressed in plain English, which is more helpful for preachers than is symbolic logic. Whatever the textbook or method, preachers must make themselves masters of the argument, not in the sense of being combative, but of following proper reasoning. Our forebears may have become proficient in grammar and logic before leaving secondary school, but we likely have some catching up to do in order to move on to rhetoric.

Rhetoric

Assuming familiarity with more recent authors, I want to continue to introduce contemporary audiences to some of my older mentors. Although I have already quoted from many of those mentioned below, here I put them in a briefly annotated list of recommended books for seminarians, ministry candidates, and pastors.

In order to keep the list as short as possible and to avoid excessive redundancy, I left out some of the less original of those previously quoted and added some others I haven't mentioned. The more recent works that made it into my list are not necessarily better than others, but they qualified because they serve to bring out the best insights about delivery from previous ages.

- Aristotle, *Rhetoric*. Although Aristotle is not the most engaging writer, he wrote the book on rhetoric, which has widely influenced Western rhetoric. He did not, however, discuss delivery. Much of what later became common stock appears in Aristotle explicitly or in seed form.
- Cicero, *On Oratory*. Cicero is enjoyable to read with his bantering dialogues, which bring Aristotle and other Greeks and Romans to life. However, it takes a little while to get into the heart of the work, and it is anything but systematic. The reader has to be attentive to hidden gems. Also, he mentioned a host of names that will be completely unknown to the modern reader (except to classics professors). However, knowledge of the persons mentioned is not necessary to benefit from their examples. Crassus is the main spokesman, but Antonius and Caesar offer excellent advice as well.
- Augustine, 4th book of *De Doctrina Christiana*. This final chapter was Augustine's making peace

with rhetoric. Because he had been saved out of making a "sale of loquacity,"[20] he stood at a distance from rhetoric for a long time after his conversion, wanting to be a Christian, not a Ciceronian. All the while, he *practiced* rhetoric in his widely acclaimed sermons. He wrote the first three chapters of this book early on, covering questions of interpretation. He finished it toward the end of his life, adding this final chapter on sermon delivery, deciding that it was better that truth be as well clothed as is error.

- François Fénelon, *Dialogues on Eloquence*. In the tradition of the dialogues of Cicero, Fénelon delightfully traced a conversation among three interlocutors. Concerned about the poor state of Roman Catholic preaching in France, he wanted more biblical preaching and more extemporaneous preaching. Shorter than Cicero, this dialogue gets into the main topic right away and is surprisingly relevant for contemporary Protestant preachers as well.

- Richard Whately, *Elements of Rhetoric.* Whately, like many of his peers, followed a simplified version of the faculty psychology, dividing the human being into intellect and will. Part I is about arguments addressed to the intellect and really falls more under logic than rhetoric. Part II covers arguments addressed to the will, analyzing the feelings of the hearers. Part III is about perspicuity, elegance, and energy of style. If readers want to jump right to his original analysis of the differences between reading

and speaking, they can profitably go directly to Part IV, which covers delivery.
- James Garretson, *Princeton and Preaching*. Garretson's work offers a warm discussion of fascinating original research of Archibald Alexander's papers in the Princeton Seminary archives. He uncovered for us how this great extemporaneous preacher delivered sermons and taught homiletics.
- James Alexander, *Thoughts on Preaching*. These unsystematic thoughts and letters are delightful gems on many aspects of preaching, including three letters to pastoral candidates about extemporaneous preaching.
- Adolphe Monod, "The Delivery of Sermons." In this brief article, Monod discussed the three delivery methods, addressed the question of why public speaking is so difficult, and got to the heart of the answer, which is a question of faith (as I described in Chapter 2).
- Henry Ware, Jr., *Hints on Extemporaneous Preaching*. Because Ware was a Unitarian, he is understandably unknown and overlooked by Christian homileticians, but his short work presents excellent recommendations for extemporaneous address and does not actively promote heretical theology.
- Charles Spurgeon, *Lectures to My Students*. Spurgeon covered many aspects of gospel ministry, especially preaching, in an entertainingly engaging and witty manner.
- Robert Dabney, *Lectures on Sacred Rhetoric*. As mentioned in the introduction, Dabney was the one

who opened up to me the riches of classical rhetoric and nineteenth-century homiletics. Dabney combined the best thoughts of the ages with practical instruction for students. His writing style is often strident, but overlooking the tone will pay rich dividends.

- D. Martyn Lloyd-Jones, *Preaching and Preachers*. Lloyd-Jones gave these lectures at Westminster Theological Seminary. They are theoretically sound, practically useful, and continually relevant. He strongly advocated extemporaneous preaching.
- Edmund Clowney, *Preaching and Biblical Theology*. Strictly speaking, this work does not fit in this list, because it is not about delivery. However, I include it because Dr. Clowney was the one who first introduced me to the glories of Christ-centered, redemptive historical preaching, without which the most powerful delivery will amount to little.

In sum, as part of a lifelong effort to become better speakers, we can improve by reading good books, writing often, listening to good speakers, and mastering grammar, logic, and rhetoric. From learning, we now turn to practice, which makes, if not perfect, at least better.

Practice Speaking Constantly

We all practice extemporaneous speech every day, but we do not necessarily take advantage of our quotidian conversations to improve our speech. Dabney offered several pieces of advice in this regard, recommending first that preachers should practice making every utterance, even in normal conversation, "a drill in correctness of speech." He clarified:

> You will, of course, not apprehend me as inciting you to the affectation of clothing our familiar converse in stilted and pedantic phrase: this would be silly in the pulpit also; but you should speak always clearly and properly, allowing in yourself no grammatical errors, no slouched and involuntary forms of expression.[21]

Furthermore, the preacher should practice extemporaneous speech daily if possible, addressed only to the trees if necessary, not in order to practice an upcoming sermon but to practice speaking fluently, grammatically, simply, and logically.[22] While I do not address the trees, I often address the interior of my car as I am driving or the wall in front of my desk, not composing entire speeches but talking through issues that are in my mind or sticky points in the upcoming sermon.

Spurgeon recommended just such a practice:

> Thought is to be linked with speech; that is the problem; and it may assist a man in its solution, if he endeavours in his private musings to think aloud. So has this become habitual to me that I find it very helpful to be able, in private devotion, to pray with my voice; reading aloud is more beneficial to me than the silent process; and when I am mentally working out a sermon, it is a relief to me to speak to myself as the thoughts flow forth.[23]

This is different from practicing the whole sermon aloud, since the purpose of thinking aloud is not so much to practice oratory as to check logical flow to see if something makes sense. If I have trouble composing words to explain my ideas, it is an indication that my ideas are still half-baked. Better to discover this confusion while driving in my car or sitting at my desk than while standing before the congregation. Along these lines, one of my colleagues, Dr. Tim Sansbury, emphasized the utility of working especially through transitions out loud, since, as he said, "sometimes they seem like they will be easy until I try to do them."[24]

Dabney strongly rejected the advice of some homileticians to practice before a mirror or even to declaim the whole sermon out loud in preparation for the preaching. His objection was that these exercises are necessarily artificial in the absence of an audience and will only serve to throw off the best intuitions of the preacher in the moment of preaching by suggesting the previously and artificially selected words and movements. Convinced of the power of the rhetorical moment to dictate proper speech and action, Dabney warned, "If you attempt by such means to decide in advance precisely how this particular sentence, or that, is to be delivered, you will assuredly decide ill; because it is a matter which can only be well decided by the natural impulse of the moment."[25]

In my very earliest attempts at preaching, I tried to practice my sermons, even a few times in front of a mirror. While I cannot dictate what works for others, not only did I feel ridiculous, but I was also patently artificial, so I soon abandoned the practice. Still, I find it very helpful to talk through parts of my sermon to make sure I can speak my ideas smoothly and concisely.

Dabney also urged his charges to take such real opportunities for public speech as they were offered. Finding opportunities for real public speaking is a significant problem for seminarians, especially in lands where trained pastors abound. Who wants to hear the neophyte when the master is available? Seminarians can graduate without ever having preached in a church.

In Mexico and in much of the world, this is not as much of a problem, since pastors are scarce, and candidates are often thrust into positions before they are prepared. In our work in Guadalajara, we had one or two ordained pastors and five sites, one with multiple services in two languages, so elders and candidates regularly preached. (Here is another plug for missionary service. If you want to have ample opportunities to develop as a preacher, become a missionary.)

In places with an abundance of preachers, the experienced pastors and the churches themselves need to take on the preparation of the next generation of pastors as a principal responsibility. The reality is that the preachers of today will soon be gone. Therefore, accomplished preachers need to make time in their work for coaching aspiring candidates—helping them to prepare, listening to their sermons, encouraging them constantly, and giving constructive criticism. Also, churches need to make room for candidates in public meetings in keeping with their current level and to give them opportunities to move to the next level. Years ago, a young candidate preached a powerful sermon in our church in Mexico City, after which a member jokingly said to me, "You had better be careful, or he might take your place." The member was shocked when I replied, "That is my goal."

The transition in that church did not go well because I did not stay around long enough to prepare thoroughly for my departure. Seeing my failure, I purposed to do things differently in Guadalajara, starting from scratch and spending twenty years getting the church ready for the next generation. Actually, the church was prepared to go on without me sooner than I was ready to go on without it. Finally, I made the heart-wrenching decision to leave, in part because I knew that the people we had trained needed more space to develop, space that they would not enjoy with my shadow cast over everything.

In my return to the United States, I was surprised and distressed to see that a growing measure of pastoral success is not how many persons one has trained but how many places one can preach at the same time through technological means. Instead of multiplying themselves by training younger preachers, some preachers multiply themselves by simultaneously beaming their images to multiple sites.

As they inevitably and soon pass off the scene, it will be hard to find their replacements, and many of the aspiring young preachers who passed through their churches will have long since departed in search of training and opportunities. I once heard a gifted young man who was a "campus pastor" at one such church. However, it seemed like most of his work was setting the stage for the "lead pastor" to show up from the main campus.

When I asked this young man if the lead pastor trained him and gave him opportunities to preach, he said, "Our lead pastor is another level," apparently meaning that no one could preach as well, so it didn't make sense for anyone else to try as long as the master was around. That site eventually closed down, and the gifted young man is now selling real estate. While selling real estate is a good occupation, I wonder what he might be doing now if a seasoned pastor had invested in him and given him opportunities to preach.

Classroom Exercises

Taking advantage of the assigned readings in a preaching course, instructors can kill two or more birds with one stone by doing evaluations orally. That is, instructors can have the students explain in brief oral presentations what they learned from their reading, sometimes using complete manuscripts, sometimes using outlines, and sometimes with no notes at all. It is good to have a timer ready so students learn to manage their time.

As the program progresses, one can include more assignments with outlines only or without notes. This procedure will also keep the instructor from having to read dull book reviews. In addition to these assignments for which the topic is known beforehand, instructors can include frequent, brief, extemporaneous explanations of topics announced in the moment and delivered by students chosen at random on the spot. For example, out of nowhere, an instructor could ask three students to give a three-minute address on climate change or marijuana legalization or the death penalty or any other topic that would require some fast mental scrambling to formulate something coherent to say. As the students advance in their studies, one could include biblical texts or theological or practical topics. For example, the instructor could ask three students to explain short sections of Romans.

Also, one could use the same procedure to respond to audio or video recordings of representative speeches, not necessarily sermons. For example, the students could listen to a speech by Winston Churchill, Ronald Reagan, or Jesse Jackson and respond in three minutes to the oration, or they could try to repeat a key part of the speech in their own words. After each student gives a speech, the class can point out strong points and aspects that need improving, and the instructor can add comments at the end. The students will likely be gentle with each other, knowing that their turn is coming next.

If an educational institution has close relationships with local churches, it can work to obtain opportunities for students to give brief exhortations and later, entire lessons or sermons to groups at the church or to the entire congregation. Churches could function, for example, like mariachi groups, which are set up like trades with masters and apprentices. In a mariachi group, everyone gets to play, from the least experienced novice to the most accomplished virtuoso, but each at his or her level. Also, the more experienced have a responsibility to bring the less experienced along. Churches could let the nervous student read a Scripture text one Sunday, previously tutored by the pastor about how to read in public. Later, the student could make a two-minute comment on a text that is complementary to the main text to be preached that day. Next, the church could invite the student to give a lesson to the seniors' luncheon or to the youth group or to the children's class. As progress becomes evident, the leadership could invite the student to preach a sermon at the evening or mid-week service and later in the main service.

In a community where there is a seminary, there may be a glut of respected professors, accomplished pastors, and lowly seminarians. Even if churches are fulfilling their responsibility to train up the next generation, there still may not be enough opportunities for seminarians to develop their skills. Therefore, people could create a forum open to students, professors, pastors, and the public in which students can give brief lectures and receive feedback. To attract people from the community in addition to the students' mothers, short lectures by professors or popular pastors on relevant topics could be a draw. As in a concert in which newer bands warm up the audience for the main act, the students could prepare the hearers for the experienced teachers. As the students progress, the masters could be the warm-up act for the students.

Colleges and seminaries often have their presidents or most skilled professors give public lectures in order to recruit students who want to study under such gifted teachers (and to attract donors who will help pay for them). However, these teachers are not the most appropriate role models for the potential students, unless the schools hope to produce mostly professors. More impressive and more to the point would be for the schools to put forward some of their best students, whom potential students could realistically aspire to imitate (and who would showcase for potential donors the real "products" of the schools). This approach can backfire, of course, as it did when a recent graduate suddenly lost his voice right before he was supposed to speak at a gathering that I attended for alumni of my seminary. His sudden laryngitis was surprising since his voice was working just fine earlier in the evening. Even if the young man's courage failed him in the moment, I had to admire the courage of the seminary in putting him forward in the first place and was sorry we didn't get to hear him speak.

Even if churches do not open their ministries up to students, open-air preaching can provide another opportunity to preach, and no invitation is required, although a permit may be. This idea will unsettle many and may not be practical or advisable in many circumstances. However, it should not be dismissed out of hand, since it has a noble history dating back to Old Testament times and running through the New Testament and church history (reviewed and recommended by Spurgeon in his chapters

17 and 18 of *Lectures to My Students*). I have seen and heard preachers ranting on street corners and calling down damnation on passers-by, which is generally enough to close most people to the idea of open-air preaching. A few years ago, I was in Chattanooga, Tennessee, during the city's River Fest. There was a group of men and boys announcing judgment on the merry families strolling along. I stayed within earshot for a while to see if they ever mentioned Christ, which they eventually did, though ever so briefly. It was a disturbing encounter.

The way we preached on the street during seminary days was to position ourselves where people were waiting for public transportation and had a few minutes to spare. One student would preach a very brief gospel message, while companions distributed themselves throughout the crowd. After the brief message, the companions would turn to others and ask them what they thought of what the preacher had just said. Sometimes good conversations would ensue. Occasionally one of the seminarians would launch a question to the preacher, which would engage the crowd. I cannot say how we came across, but we always tried to be respectful and friendly with the commuters. As I already mentioned, the main benefit was probably not had by the hearers but by the would-be preachers.

Work With the Bible

For those who are instructing future preachers, another exercise that has more to do with exegesis than delivery is the division of books of the Bible into preaching units. I do not ever remember having to do this in seminary, but it is an essential skill for the expository preacher. Teachers can have students develop calendars of sermons, dividing books of the Bible into units of varying lengths, in the process forcing them into uncomfortable requirements. For example, first have them develop a calendar for a six-month series on Romans. When they are finished, ask them to develop a six-week series on Romans, reminding them that the original audience likely heard the letter read in one sitting. If they insist that the series must be longer, have them prepare a sixteen-week series, but on Titus. The purpose is not to irritate the students but to force them to discover natural breaks in the flow of the books, identifying larger units and smaller ones. As they work with many books of the Bible, they will begin to see these natural divisions automatically. Of course, no instructor or classroom is necessary, as preachers can do this exercise on their own and will do so regularly if they preach series through entire books of the Bible.

In addition to dividing whole books into units, preachers will benefit from developing syntactical outlines of the individual units. One simple method is to copy and paste the text into a word processor and use indents, highlights, underlining, italics, bold, and colors to bring out the structure of the text, noting transitions, repetitions, clarifications, amplifications, parallels, contrasts, breaks, etc. When I have demonstrated this simple method, people are sometimes amazed at what comes out —an outline that lends itself to clear and concise preaching. Once I worked on Hebrews 1 with a group of experienced church leaders, and they were surprised at the simplicity of the text once its structure became clear, deciding that they could preach a two-point sermon: 1) Jesus is superior to the prophets. 2) Jesus is superior to the angels. Constant diagraming of texts will give students and preachers a keen eye for the development of thoughts, and they will eventually find themselves analyzing the structure of every text they read.

Sermon Outlining

Often seminaries have their students write out full sermon manuscripts, and I agree that writing helps us to grow in our ability to use words well. However, first we need to be able to write sermon outlines because the outlines reveal the structure. If a person suffers from scoliosis (curvature of the spine), when he or she is fully dressed, the condition may be invisible. If the person were seen in a swimming suit, the curvature may be more noticeable. However, it would be most visible in an X-ray of the skeleton. The sermon outline is the skeleton of the sermon. All dressed up in a complete manuscript, an improper structure may not be apparent, but presented alone it has nowhere to hide.

A well-structured sermon outline allows the preacher to see at a glance the structure of the entire sermon, and the key to a good outline is proper hierarchy. Statements to the left are bigger ideas than those to the right, which are subordinate to and support the bigger idea to the left. Also, statements at the same level should have the same level of importance. That is, they should be roughly parallel. I say, "roughly parallel," because we mostly want to follow the text, which may not fit into any neat scheme.

Also, the outline should have forward movement, taking the preacher and the people along the path of the text. Sometimes people complain about sermons that did not move them, and their complaint is just, but perhaps not in the way they mean. A sermon should indeed move people by advancing their understanding, devotion, and commitment from where they were at the beginning of the sermon toward where the text says they should be. A sermon outline that moves forward along the rails of the text is more likely to move the preacher and the congregation forward in their minds, hearts, and wills.

There are some who object to the imposition of any outline on the text because of the danger of distorting the meaning of the text. Because of this danger, it is best to learn to make syntactical outlines of the text before making homiletical outlines for preaching the sermon. In most cases, they will be basically the same outline. The main difference is that the homiletical outline adds necessary information and brings in application appropriate to the contemporary audience.

After many years of mostly informal training of preachers, I had the opportunity to teach a seminary course called "Preparation and Delivery of Sermons," in which I largely followed the plan laid out in this chapter, although I could not assign all of the recommended works to read. It was remarkable to observe how the students developed in their extemporaneous ability over only one semester of weekly oral exercises. They also grew in their sense of how to structure a sermon and their ability to notice solid historical connections between the Old Testament and the New.

The final assignments included a twelve-week series of sermon outlines on Philippians, one redemptive-historical sermon outline from an Old Testament text, and one recorded sermon or lesson delivered in a real setting. One student preached his in the seminary chapel as his senior sermon (a sermon by those soon to graduate) and received positive feedback from the faculty members, who were impressed by his improvement over earlier efforts. The students reported that they felt liberated in their preaching and, although not nearly as polished as when reading, they connected with the hearers noticeably better. One felt that he had failed because of his untidy speaking and was shocked to find people coming up to him afterwards with tears in their eyes to thank him. The students' experience was beyond what I had hoped or imagined could happen so quickly. They had tasted something of the joy and the effectiveness of combining thorough preparation with free speech.

People often ask me how I learned to speak Spanish. I can tell them of the two years in high school, one semester at a community college, and nine months in language school, but I emphasize twenty-four years of living in Mexico. I also say that I'm continuing to learn it. In other words, the only way to learn to speak a language is to speak that language. Similarly, the only way to learn to preach is to preach. More accurately, the only way to learn to preach well is to preach better and better all the time. My hope is that there is something in these pages to help you to preach better so that you will end up preaching well.

---

1. Ian Duguid, "Tell Me the Old, Old Story," in Rhett Dodson, ed., *Unashamed Workmen*, 82.
2. Cicero, *On Oratory and Orators*, 255; bk. 3, ch. 56.
3. Cicero, *On Oratory and Orators*, 214; bk. 3, ch. 20.
4. Cicero, *On Oratory and Orators*, 228; bk. 3, ch. 31.
5. Cicero, *On Oratory and Orators*, 34; bk. 1, ch. 25.
6. Cicero, *On Oratory and Orators*, 34; bk. 1, ch. 25.
7. C. R. Vaughn*, ed., Discussions of Robert Lewis Dabney*, 3 vols. 1891 (Carlisle: The Banner of Truth Trust, 1967), 2: 37.
8. Dabney, *Sacred Rhetoric*, 7.
9. Fénelon, 86.
10. Dabney, *Sacred Rhetoric*, 339
11. Dabney, *Sacred Rhetoric,* 339.
12. Spurgeon, 141.
13. Fénelon, 115.
14. *Great Speeches of the 20th Century* (Los Angeles: Rhino Records, Inc., 1991).
15. Dabney, *Sacred Rhetoric*, 323.

16. Louis Bautain, *The Art of Extempore Speaking*, 1858 (New York: Blue Ribbon Books, 1940), 23.
17. Bautain, 41.
18. Bautain, 42.
19. Spurgeon, 331.
20. Augustine, *The Confessions*. trans. Edward B. Pusey, in *Augustine,* Vol. 18 of Great Books of the Western World. ed. Robert Maynard Hutchins (Chicago: Encyclopedia Britannica, Inc., 1952), 19; 4. 2. 2.
21. Dabney, *Sacred Rhetoric*, 340.
22. Dabney, *Sacred Rhetoric,* 340–41.
23. Spurgeon, 149.
24. From a personal communication on October 14, 2021.
25. Dabney, *Sacred Rhetoric,* 327.

Chapter 5
Don't Try This at Home

It could be that some candidates for the ministry and preachers reading this book are ready to try their hand at greater extemporaneity, perhaps reducing the size of their sermon notes or dispensing with them altogether. Lest I be guilty of unleashing worse preaching on the church, I would like to add some cautionary notes, dissuading some preachers from attempting this method, or at least offering safeguards to protect it from abuse. Referring to extemporaneous delivery, Monod cautioned:

> I believe, indeed, that this is the method in which one may hope for the best delivery; provided, always, that the speaker has so great a facility, or so complete a preparation, or what is better, both at once, as to be freed from the necessity of a painful search for thoughts and words. Without this, it is the worst of all methods, for matter as well as for form.[1]

I assume that other preachers have the same experience as I do, that the people who (in our opinion) most need to hear a certain sermon are not present when we preach it, and those who least need to hear it are present. On the Lord's Day in which our text includes Hebrews 10:25's warning against neglecting assembling together, we have the lowest attendance of the year. Only the most faithful are present. When our text in 1 Timothy 6 contains clear and challenging instructions for the rich, the wealthiest members are on a trip to the islands.

The opposite can happen as well, when people are present at what seems like just the wrong time. For example, after years of inviting our neighbors to church, I was horrified when they showed up on the only Sunday in several years in which I was preaching specifically about money.

I fear the same could happen here. Some preachers whom I would most like to encourage to be more extemporaneous are likely to be the ones who will avoid the practice, and others who have already rushed headlong into the practice would do well to pull back and stick to fuller manuscripts.

In general, I would like to encourage my colleagues who are the most careful in their preparation to be more spontaneous in their delivery. Also, I would like to encourage my colleagues who are known for readiness of speech to devote more time to preparation and tighten up their delivery with more written material. Going against the grain of the rest of this book, this chapter is a warning against bad tendencies that we preachers often have and that the extemporaneous method makes worse. I hope that it also provides some helpful suggestions about remedies to avoid these pitfalls, for the problem is not the method but the messenger. Specifically, I recommend that we all install some early warning alarms in our heads in order to avoid the vices that are too common in extemporaneous addresses.

A Warning to the Negligent

James Alexander admitted:

> The resulting fact is, that in numberless instances, the extemporaneous preacher neglects his preparation. If he has begun in the slovenly way while still young, and before he had laid up stores of knowledge, he will, in nine cases out of ten, be a shallow, rambling sermonizer as long as he lives.[2]

Dabney gave one of the sternest warnings to extemporaneous preachers, which is worth quoting at length:

> The great danger which attends the *extempore* preacher is that he will, after a time, abuse his facility. The capacity for fluent speech is one which is very easily expanded after the first successes. The multifarious avocations of the pastor often furnish a pretext for self-indulgence, and tempt to the neglect both of general study and special preparation. The fluent declaimer can, for a time, cover his deficiency of matter by his readiness of speech. He avails himself of this unlucky resort, and further indulges his indolence. His fecundity of mind is lost, his freshness is exhaled, he gradually comes to that final state in which the mind can do nothing but run the dull round of its little circle of commonplaces. Whatever may be the text, the sermon is substantially the same. The Church presents but too many illustrations of this danger. They are sad, and should be awakening to our souls. You see here and there those clerical drones who have long ceased to interest or control any one, and who are only endured by churches who are dying by inches under their charge; yet those who are older

than you can remember the bright auspices under which these very men began their ministry. Fluent, animated and energetic, they were followed by admiring crowds; their preaching seemed to be blessed of God; their friends prophesied for them a splendid career. But they learned gradually to abuse their facility, and to relax their studies: the end is what you see. The young minister might well pray, were it lawful, that a premature death might cut him down in this auspicious springtime, rather than that he should reach his autumn, only to disgrace his early promise by this crime.[3]

There are times in pastoral ministry when we must fall back on all our prior preparation, because a series of emergencies fills up our weeks, and we truly do not have enough time to prepare as we ought. Also, it is always true that we could have studied more, and we may realize while we are preaching that we did leave some stones unturned. However, if sloth becomes a habit, then we are in serious danger, a danger that Dabney called worse than death.

My early warning alarms are to help me avoid shipwreck in my ministry. For example, if I sense that a humorous comment that occurs to me at a dinner gathering would be inappropriate, I want a warning alarm to go off before it slips out. If I detect that a greeting with a woman is a little too friendly, I want a bell to sound. If I am preaching, and I find that I have left a large stone unturned—an important word, a significant reference, a rich allusion, a sticky syntactical question—and I am tempted to cover my negligence by fluency or speculation, I want a loud clanging to sound in my mind (since I myself am at risk of becoming a loud clanging). If I have skimped on preparation and am standing in the pulpit, it is too late for me to teach on that text as I should, but I want to avoid adding insult to injury by pretending to teach on it by putting words together that form a subterfuge to cover my omission. Better to go back later and study the overlooked aspects of the text for my own benefit and as a benefit for future hearers. It is essential that occasional negligence not become a fixed habit.

An indication that eloquent negligence has already become a habit is the repetition of phrases, expressions, or stories. When your preaching begins to sound like Rewind-Play, something is seriously wrong. If I am away from my own church on the Lord's Day (which I try to avoid), I worship at a local congregation wherever I am. I had the experience of visiting the same church twice with exactly a year between the two visits, pastored by a man with a reputation as an extemporaneous preacher. On both occasions, he told a story about himself, and on both occasions, it was the very same story. He also repeated the same expressions, which seemed to be stock phrases for him. I wonder if he had discovered nothing new to teach God's people, or if he had not prepared adequately, or if he was simply hitting Rewind and Play.

Install the Rewind-Play Alarm in your head, and put it on the most sensitive setting. To make sure it works properly, ask trusted friends in your congregation if you are recycling old material or repeating commonplaces. We need to be aware of favorite phrases, illustrations, stories, authors, or quotations. Even the best preachers have stock phrases. Charles Spurgeon often and very conveniently heard someone saying exactly what he wanted to answer, which he introduced with, "Do I hear someone saying?" He also loved to repeat the lines from "Rock of Ages" by Augustus Toplady, "Nothing in my hand I bring, Simply to thy cross I cling." For some preachers, every sermon seems to be about "idols of the heart" or the need to "preach the Gospel to yourself" or "love for the city." For others, sermons require a well-worn quotation from C. S. Lewis or another famous author. Others constantly mention references from popular culture. The worst form of recycling is plagiarism, which is preaching all or part of someone else's sermons as if it were one's own

If you have a long ministry in one place and return to Bible books that you have already preached, do not simply pull out your old notes and reuse them. Every four or five years in Guadalajara, I did a series on Romans, since we had new people all the time, and the long-standing members never tired of it. Also, over two decades of hearing expository preaching, the congregation grew tremendously in what it could handle, giving me the challenge and the freedom to go deeper into the details of the text each time around.

I tried to make a practice of not consulting my old notes at all or at least not until I had mostly finished preparing my new ones. One year, in addition to being the pastor of the church, I added two jobs that had been full-time for the previous persons—Mexico country director for our mission, and interim director of our school. It was a miserable time and the busiest of my life. For a short series of four weeks on Colossians, I pulled out my old notes and preached from them, feeling like I was shortchanging the congregation and myself.

In contrast, as I preached through Romans four times over twenty years, preparing fresh sermons, I was amazed and encouraged by how much I learned each time. I was also embarrassed at how much I had missed the previous times through. In order for our congregations to keep growing, we preachers need to keep growing in our exegetical ability, no matter how spontaneously eloquent we become.

By the way, if I preach at another church, I often use sermons that I have already preached in my own. Even so, if I do not go back and do at least a little spade work, I sometimes find that my sermon notes do not make enough sense in the moment of preaching from them. If I composed complete sermon manuscripts, I would not face this problem, but my two or three pages that made so much sense to me when I first used them can grow more opaque with time. I mention this tendency in order to warn against too facile a recycling of sermon notes without some prior preparation, even if the hearers are new to the material.

I have not been the pastor of many churches, so I had not faced the question of what to preach in a new church until fairly recently. As we were packing up to move back to the United States from Mexico, we gave away or threw away many things. I finally disposed of my handwritten seminary notes after thirty years of preserving them. I also had my own sermon and lecture notes to consider.

Although I did not dispose of them, I left them all in Mexico, leaving the eventual task of disposing them to someone else. Of course, I can still consult many of my notes in digital form, but I am less tempted to do so if they are not physically beside me in a filing cabinet. All congregations need to hear the most recent results of their pastors' ever-deepening exegetical skills rather than yesterday's best conclusions warmed over.

A Warning to the Verbose

Decades ago I knew a man who was certain that he was called to be a preacher, and one of his primary advantages, according to him, was his "don de la palabra" or gift of gab. He spoke incessantly, at length, quickly, and with conviction. For some reason, he thought that this was what pastors do. The problem was that he generally provoked a negative reaction in others, although he was oblivious to their boredom or irritation. At the other extreme, I have known men who were so painfully shy or socially awkward that they could scarcely carry on normal conversations, but they felt called to the ministry as well.

Neither of these extreme personalities seems to me to be the best type for pastoral ministry, but I have observed that some of the best preachers are those that tend to be on the quiet side. They do not force their way into conversations, but when they speak, people listen. Their sermons tend to be modest in length, full of content because of excellent preparation and the use of exactly the right words and only those. Writing and reading sermon manuscripts can help produce this effect, in part because these activities permit preachers to find the best language to express their thoughts. Also, writing is so laborious and reading aloud so taxing to the voice that these activities normally encourage us to be concise. However, extemporaneous preachers must also work to achieve an economy of words.

When we dropped off our younger daughter at college in West Palm Beach, we attended a new church led by Jeremy McKeen. Under his enthusiastic leading and preaching, the church grew rapidly over the next four years. I began listening to his sermons and giving him feedback, which he accepted very well, telling me that if he wanted only praise, he would consult his mother. After listening to several sermons, I told him that I would evaluate only ones that did not go over forty minutes. A few years after I stopped coaching him, I had the privilege of visiting his church and hearing him preach an excellent sermon, chock-full of content, well-organized, appropriately passionate, focused on the text and on Christ, and under my forty-minute limit. He was already a fine preacher, and I contributed relatively little to his development, but I may deserve some thanks from his congregation for pushing him toward greater conciseness.

I was heartened to find that Spurgeon agreed with this outside limit, even though he was one of the most gifted extemporaneous orators of the church and lived in an age in which longer speeches were likely more tolerated. With his characteristic wit, he said:

> In order to maintain attention, *avoid being too long*. An old preacher used to say to a young man who preached an hour, – "My dear friend, I do not care what else you preach about, but I wish you would always preach *about* forty minutes." We ought seldom to go much beyond that – forty minutes, or, say, three quarters of an hour. If a fellow cannot say all he has to say in that time, when will he say it? But somebody said he liked "to do justice to his subject." Well, but ought he not to do justice to his people, or, at least, have a little mercy upon them, and not keep them too long? The subject will not complain of you, but the people will.[4]

Cultural norms vary, and congregations vary, so no hard rule is possible. Also, individual sermons vary. I generally plan for a half hour, am relaxed if it extends to thirty-five minutes, and try to maintain forty minutes as a cut-off time. However, I have recently preached some sermons that lasted around fifty minutes and kept the attention of the congregation the whole time. By the way, I do not have a clock visible while I preach, in order to avoid imposing artificial limitations on the sermon. After decades, my internal clock is fairly accurate, but I know with precision how long the sermon was only after it is over. By reading the congregation, I also know if it seemed short or long, which is more important than its actual length.

During my most wretched sermons, after finding no way to rescue them, I have hastened to conclude, out of mercy for the congregation and to relieve myself of the misery of continuing. These sermons seemed intolerably long to everyone. At other times, when the Spirit seemed to be taking over, I went with the flow and continued for considerably longer than I had anticipated. These sermons seemed to take no time at all.

In general, very few will complain of your sermons being too short. The best situation is when people comment that a sermon *seemed* short, even though it had been at least normal length. One of my professors (I cannot recall at this moment if it was Dr. Clowney or Dr. Keller, so I mention them both) gave us instructions about visiting people in their homes. He said for us to leave while they still want us to stay. I have extended that prudent principle to many areas of ministry, including preaching. Stop preaching while they still want you to continue. If they later remark that they wanted you to keep going, tell them that you will, Lord willing, at the next meeting.

In this regard, extemporaneous preachers have a distinct advantage over those who recite or read a manuscript. Instead of reading a manuscript, preachers can focus on reading the congregation because they are looking at them most of the time. Also, they can more easily adjust the content of their message, while those following a manuscript will have a harder time reducing or expanding material on the spot without ruining the flow of the sermon.

When I preach, I know that I am dependent for the effectiveness of the sermon on my preparation, on the Holy Spirit, and on the congregation. As I look at the congregation throughout the sermon, I am constantly making mid-course adjustments not only to the content but also to the volume, rapidity, tone, and length.

In Mexico, I had the advantage of preaching multiple times on the Lord's Day to distinct congregations, first in English and then twice or three times in Spanish. As I saw the English-speaking congregation grow attentive at one point and become listless and distracted at another, I took note and made immediate adjustments and also changes for the Spanish sermons.

Did I lose them with the long supplementary Scripture reading? I summarized it the next time. Did my illustration fall flat or produce quizzical looks? I found another one or eliminated it altogether. Did my application hit home? I asked myself how it would work in the other language and culture. Again, the capital advantage of extemporaneous preaching is that we are speaking to people and making the normal and natural adaptations that such speaking demands and affords.

Spurgeon went on to identify a common cause of lengthy sermons—insufficient preparation:

> If you ask me how you may shorten your sermons, I should say, *study them better*. Spend more time in the study that you may need less in the pulpit. We are generally longest when we have least to say. A man with a great deal of well-prepared matter will probably not exceed forty minutes; when he has less to say he will go on to fifty minutes, and when he has absolutely nothing he will need an hour to say it in.[5]

Another cause of lengthy preaching is taking each section of the text not as an integral part of the whole text but as a springboard to talk about the various topics that are directly or indirectly suggested by each section. In the nineteenth century, the common approach was to take an isolated text and preach on its main topic. While a steady diet of this approach tends to produce Christians who are more knowledgeable about the Bible's doctrines than the Bible itself, it can be useful to use small texts to explore topics. Of course, knowledge of the Bible's doctrines and knowledge of the Bible itself are not mutually exclusive. They represent the complementary disciplines of Systematic Theology and Biblical Theology, respectively.

A prominent pastor once spoke to us seminarians about the four sermons he preached on John 11:35, *"Jesus wept."* I cannot remember all the details, but one of the sermons was on the humanity of Jesus, another on the tenderness of Jesus, and so on. He was a very good preacher, and no doubt they were excellent messages, but they had to have been useful lessons on Christology more than expositions of the tiny text. Also, none of these four sermons necessarily had to be overly long. However, when a preacher uses a similar procedure with the various sections of the text, it tends to produce long sermons.

At first, this approach to preaching sounds like really digging into the text, but it is more a collection of topical mini-sermons. The tendency of this type of sermon is to multiply biblical references, reporting on many or all of the verses that treat the same word or theme. Not only does this approach often neglect to explain the text as it stands in its context, but it also tends to be long.

On vacation, our family had the pleasure of visiting a nearby church. The preacher treated a portion of Romans 9 section by section. He clearly explained the doctrines taught in the text and illuminated them with many references to other Scriptures. The pastor did a fine job teaching the important doctrines, but at the end of the forty-five minutes, I had not heard much about the text in its context. Although I strongly recommend preaching through books of the Bible as the normal practice, if we preach at times about a doctrine or other topic, we can learn from our nineteenth-century forebears to choose a small text and focus on one topic per sermon.

Dabney identified another cause of verbosity, the power of the rhetorical moment. In fact, he considered that the first serious difficulty for the extemporaneous preacher "is to make his words scarce." So overwhelmingly powerful is the rhetorical moment that it actually suggests to the preacher words that are too many and too complicated:

> You will find (what you may not now suppose) that abundant verbiage will come to you in *extempore* speech with far more facility than the direct, apt and simple structure, and that your constant temptation will be to employ the former for hiding and supplementing your poverty in regard to the latter. You will be tempted to pour out forty words, because you cannot, as you are conscious you ought to do, express the thought in twelve. In a word, the great difficulty in the way of *extempore* eloquence is to avoid verbal redundancy, and to make the style compact, nervous and clear.[6]

Dabney went on to observe that the unskilled preacher can construct complicated sentences with ease because these always provide multiple means of grammatically correct escape. However, the simple and direct sentence demands a correct conclusion and demands it immediately. Therefore, simple utterance is the greater accomplishment.[7]

For example, if I begin a sentence with, "In our search for clarity and in an effort to avoid obfuscation, we find it incumbent on ourselves to distill the essence of the present verse, having considered heretofore its immediate and wider contexts, and looking forward in anticipation to what follows," I could go on and on piling up complicated subordinate clauses without every saying anything about the main point of the verse (before running out of air). However, if I start a sentence with, "The main point of this verse is," I had better find a brief way to state the main point right away.

My own experience confirms the power of the rhetorical moment to move the preacher in one of three directions. Sometimes, as Dabney noted, it suggests to me too many words. On other occasions, I have also noticed that unusual words, or complicated words, or technical ones come to me, which catch me by surprise because they are not ones I use in my everyday speech. Somehow, the moment elevates my language but so much so that I need to struggle to find the simpler word instead of the more impressive one. Best of all, at times I find that exactly the right words come to me, much clearer than the ones lying on my two or three pages of sermon notes. In those moments, no one is more surprised than I at the exactness, elegance, and power of the expressions that come out of my mouth.

I have another alarm installed, one that goes off when I am using filler words, continuing to speak when I am not sure what to say. I am merely treading water but not advancing toward the shore. I recommend that you install the Filler Alarm and ask a trusted friend to tip you off when he or she hears you filling space with needless words or using repetition that does not advance the idea. Blisteringly, Spurgeon observed:

> My brethren, it is a hideous gift to possess, to be able to say nothing at extreme length. Elongated nonsense, paraphrastic platitude, wire-drawn common-place, or sacred rodomontade [empty boasting], are common enough, and are the scandal and shame of extemporising. Even when sentiments of no value are beautifully expressed, and neatly worded, what is the use of them? Out of nothing comes nothing.[8]

I rarely listen to my recorded sermons, but we preachers can take advantage of audio or video technology to see where we are guilty of developing this "hideous gift." However, if we do listen to ourselves, we need to beware of being either mesmerized by the sound of our own voices or overly appalled at our manifest shortcomings.

A Warning to Large Personalities

Let's be honest. The pulpit offers an almost unique opportunity for self-promotion and self-indulgence. Where else can people count on an audience to address at least weekly, an audience that in some sense has to be there? That is, the people have to be there because it is their church, because they have made commitments as members, because it has always been their family's church, or because it is where they worship God and meet with friends.

They may or may not be present primarily to hear the preacher, but the preacher still takes center stage, especially in churches in which the sermon is the single biggest element of the worship service. The church provides a venue in which we preachers can be tempted to shine, to show how clever, spiritual, witty, intellectual, humble, or eloquent we are. Perhaps no method of preaching lends itself more to showing off than does the extemporaneous. Those who read or recite full manuscripts also can show off, but the impression they leave is different, since it is obvious to all that they are delivering words previously chosen and carefully crafted. They impress as good writers and dramatic readers or declaimers more than as eloquent orators. Regardless of the method, all preachers can write themselves or speak themselves too much into their sermons.

James Alexander mentioned one way in which extemporaneous preachers put themselves forward: "They talk about the way in which they are preaching." He gave some contemporary examples, which have not disappeared altogether: "After a few preliminary remarks, I shall proceed to," "What I lay down shall take the form of general principles," "I come with hesitation," or "I shall be more brief on this point." Alexander counseled to "Avoid all such observations. —More generally still, avoid all that brings the speaker's personality before the hearer."[9]

The examples that Alexander mentioned can be helpful guides to the flow of the sermon or irritating distractions that call attention to the preacher, but they are mild in comparison with today's tendencies to insert overt or covert boasts about the preacher's triumphs or accomplishments, cute stories about the preacher's family, rehearsals of how the preacher came to such a brilliant conclusion, why everyone else is wrong, or exaggerated protestations of unworthiness (which, while strictly true, are generally insincere). With regard to this last fault, Dabney warned against disingenuous self-deprecation:

> This quality of diffidence should manifest itself to the hearer, but should never be the subject of the speaker's own remark; for whenever he begins to descant on his own modesty and embarrassment, every sensible hearer will conclude at once that they are assumed. Indeed, preachers should never utter anything personally apologetic, and rarely should they make any allusion to their own circumstances.... An ostentatious avowal of diffidence is always understood as a betrayal of secret pride.[10]

What I hear these days are revelations of the preacher's sinfulness, ostensibly to show that the pastor is "transparent" or "a real person." However, they bring to mind a remark said to be a favorite of former Israeli Prime Minister Golda Meir, "Don't be so humble; you're not that great."

Some preachers simply have big personalities, while others have developed them consciously or unconsciously as their pastoral personae. Unwittingly, the congregation can encourage us to develop pastoral identities by giving us positive reinforcement of our displays of extraordinary personality. There will be people in the congregation who delight in our exhibitions of talent, wit, or feigned humility. We may even swell the numbers in our churches with a magnetic personality. However, the cost for building a church around preachers' personalities is exceedingly high. In the end, it diverts the attention of preachers and of church members, making it hard for preachers to function without applause and hard for the church to function without their extraordinary preachers.

Therefore, those who have the most magnetic personalities need to be especially disciplined in their use of extemporaneous speech. Self-promotion is easy using any delivery method, so all must beware of it. With care, preachers can edit excessive self-references out of their full manuscripts, but extemporaneous preachers may find it harder not to fill their spontaneous speech with themselves.

Another alarm can be helpful to install, the I Alarm. When we find ourselves using the word "I" frequently, we should suspect system malfunction and reset our preaching to focus on Christ. I do not mean to suggest that preachers should never mention themselves, and I occasionally use personal illustrations in my sermons, although much less than I have in this book.[11] In fact, if we never mention ourselves in our sermons, we may give the impression that the text is only for the congregation and not for us.

In addition to the sounding of the I Alarm, the congregation itself can help us to determine if our self-references are appropriate or excessive, self-deprecating or self-exalting. Also, we need to be aware that even self-deprecating personal illustrations can be a way of showing off how humble we are! If, after the worship service, the people are praising us more than praising Christ, their misguided adoration can serve as a warning to us, as long as we resist becoming intoxicated by it.

There are certainly other pitfalls to avoid, but these three—negligence in preparation, verbosity, and personal promotion—are among the most common ones. Careful exegesis and manuscript or outline writing can help us to avoid them, even if we do not read or recite what we have written or even take it with us into the pulpit.

In addition, I hope that something like my alarms will work for me and be helpful to others—the Rewind-Play Alarm, the Filler Alarm, and the I Alarm. If we are going to strive to develop our spontaneous preaching ability, we must also take the necessary precautions to guard against extemporaneous speaking's worst tendencies.

---

1. Monod, 398.
2. Alexander, *Thoughts on Preaching*, 165.
3. Dabney, *Sacred Rhetoric*, 337–8.
4. Spurgeon, 134.
5. Spurgeon, 135.
6. Dabney, *Sacred Rhetoric,* 335.
7. Dabney, 336
8. Spurgeon, 152.
9. Alexander, *Thoughts on Preaching*, 16.
10. Dabney, *Sacred Rhetoric*, 151.
11. I have used personal illustrations much more in this book than I do in my preaching and found Lloyd-Jones' comments helpful in this regard. In the Preface to his *Preaching and Preachers,* he wrote: "While preaching I rarely refer to myself; but here I felt that to be impersonal would be quite wrong. So there is a good deal of personal and anecdotal element. I trust that this will be found to be helpful by way of illustration of the principles which I have tried to inculcate."

Chapter 6
What Happens When Preachers Speak

In order to highlight the orality of a sermon, let's contrast it with a lecture. When I give a lecture, I usually use an extensive outline with full sentences, and I read much of it, throwing in clarifying or amplifying ideas along the way and then returning to read more from my notes. As I alternate between reading what I have written and adding other comments, I recognize, and the students notice, that I am shifting between two different mental operations.

I try to make the transitions as smooth as possible, but my lectures will never produce the intimate level of connection with my hearers as some of my sermons do. Why do I not then extemporize my lectures by reducing the written material and increasing the spontaneous comments? A main reason is that my memory is not good enough to do so. In a lecture, the communication of information is paramount, the amount of information is vast, and its organization is my creation. I simply cannot remember everything well enough to cover it all.

In contrast, when I preach a sermon, the outline is always before me in the biblical text itself. If my notes were to be blown into the congregation, as were Archibald Alexander's, I would still have the basic outline of the sermon before me in the text. In addition, I find that the information that I studied previously is also there hanging on the verses themselves, which serve as mnemonic devices. They bring to mind the fruits of my research to be harvested during the sermon in accordance with the interaction among the text, the Holy Spirit, the congregation, and me.

Sometimes in my lecturing, I ascend to preaching. When this happens, the students often stop taking notes or reading along in the notes I've provided them. They begin looking intently at me. Also, I sometimes descend from preaching to lecturing in my sermons. I can feel my manner turn professorial and the congregation become more languid.

If a lecture focuses on the transmission of information, a sermon aims to inform, move, and persuade. It is not that teachers are unconcerned about what the students do with the information, but normally students demonstrate their mastery by taking a test or writing an essay.

When we ascend from lecturing to preaching, we are not merely giving information to be learned, although our sermons should be full of biblical instruction. Nor are we merely giving helpful advice, although our sermons should include wise application for the hearers to put in practice. Rather, we are persuading men and women to believe the Gospel and to live it out.

Describing his preaching ministry, Paul wrote, "*Therefore, knowing the fear of the Lord, we persuade others*" (2 Cor. 5:11). Peter's spontaneous, thoroughly biblical Pentecost sermon moved hearts and persuaded wills to action: "*Now when they heard this they were cut to the heart, and said to Peter and the rest of the apostles, 'Brothers, what shall we do?'"* (Acts 2:37).

D. Martyn Lloyd-Jones emphasized this element of preaching, which distinguishes it from a lecture:

> A lecture starts with a subject, and what it is concerned to do is to give knowledge and information concerning this particular subject. It appeals primarily and almost exclusively to the mind; its object is to give instruction and state facts. That is its primary purpose and function. So a lecture, again, lacks and should lack, the element of attack, the concern to do something to the listener, which is a vital element in preaching.[1]

Dabney explained how preaching does something to the listener by inciting the affections: "It is the emotions which immediately move the will. To produce volition it is not enough that the understanding be convinced, affection must also be aroused."[2] Furthermore, in order for us to arouse affection in others, we must ourselves experience it because the same principles operate in the soul of the speaker as in the souls of the hearers. Accordingly, he gave a definition of eloquence as "the emission of the soul's energy through speech."[3] Preaching, therefore, involves nothing less than a communing of the soul of the preacher with the souls of the hearers. In other words, the preacher moves the affections of the hearers by being personally moved in the moment.

That is, preaching is an oral event in which preachers deliver themselves, enlivened by the sacred text under the impulse of the Holy Spirit. They do not merely report the highest effusions of their minds produced in the calm of their study. Lloyd-Jones emphasized the oral nature of preaching by comparing the sermon also to an essay:

> A sermon is not an essay…. This is one of the points to which I was referring earlier when pointing out the danger of printing sermons and reading them. On what grounds do I say that a sermon is not an essay? I would say that by definition the style is entirely different. An essay is written to be read, a sermon is primarily to be spoken and listened to.[4]

Jeremiah graphically described the experience of preaching when he wrote: "*If I say, 'I will not mention him, or speak any more in his name,' there is in my heart as it were a burning fire shut up in my bones, and I am weary with holding it in, and I cannot*" (Jer. 20:9). Peter and John described to the Sanhedrin their internal compulsion to speak: "*But Peter and John answered them, 'Whether it is right in the sight of God to listen to you rather than to God, you must judge, for we cannot but speak of what we have seen and heard'*" (Acts 4:19–20). Paul had Jeremiah's experience in Athens: "*Now while Paul was waiting for them at Athens, his spirit was provoked within him as he saw that the city was full of idols. So he reasoned in the synagogue with the Jews and the devout persons, and in the marketplace every day with those who happened to be there*" (Acts 17:16–17). There is an urgency to preaching that demands that preachers give full vent to the Word of God that is in them.

To mention one interesting historical example of the importance of speaking sermons and the danger of not doing so, in his *The History of The Negro Church*, the African-American historian Carter Godwin Woodson attempted to explain the lack of appeal that the Presbyterian Church (my denomination) had for

Blacks. He quoted a Bishop Tanner, who wrote of the Presbyterian Church:

> It strove to lift up without coming down and while the good Presbyterian parson was writing his discourses, rounding off the sentences, the Methodist itinerant had traveled forty miles with his horse and saddle bags; while the parson was adjusting his spectacles to read his manuscript, the itinerant had given hell and damnation to his unrepentant hearers; while the disciple of Calvin was waiting to have his church completed, the disciple of Wesley took to the woods and made them reëcho with the voice of free grace, believing with Bryant, "The groves were God's first temples."[5]

As Methodists and Baptists were winning the West, too many Presbyterians were polishing their paragraphs at Princeton. Recognizing that they were failing to appeal to the masses, and in order to reintroduce more fervor into Presbyterian preaching, the General Assembly of 1849 took the odd step of passing a personal resolution that discouraged preaching with notes. Princeton Seminary professor Charles Hodge quite rightly reacted strongly to such a stricture, understanding that it attempted to require men of differing gifts to use the same method and that it would do little to change anybody's preaching. It is interesting to note that the original motion that discouraged the use of notes focused especially on "our younger ministers, and candidates for the ministry,"[6] recognizing that it is hard to teach an old dog new tricks nor is it often necessary. Had I been a delegate at the Assembly, I would have voted against the motion even though I now urge young people to develop extemporaneous speaking ability.

The error of the General Assembly seems to have been to conclude that the method that is *most likely* to do something to the preacher and to the hearers is the *only* method that will do so. There are too many historical and contemporary examples of read and recited sermons that have produced great effects in preachers and congregations for us to dismiss these methods. At the same time, it makes sense for us to develop the method of preaching that has historically been the most powerful.

Post Hoc, Ergo Propter Hoc

Returning to the contrasting experiences I described in the Introduction, the closest I have come to the communion of souls has been during extemporaneous preaching—when I forget myself and ignore my notes, when I seem to be more of a witness than a participant in the sermon, when someone else seems to be doing the preaching, and both the congregation and I are united under the Word together, feeling and thinking the same thing. Ideas have come to me that are much more concise, clear, and exegetically sound than I was able to discover in my prior study or formulate in my sermon notes. Christ has been clearly portrayed before us all as crucified and resurrected.

I may have awakened that morning with my normal sense of Lord's Day dread, wrestled with the printer to produce my final version of notes, arrived at church to find a fresh disorder left by the youth group, and begun the worship service distracted and wanting to flee. In Mexico, I did not lead worship on the days I preached, so I had an opportunity to be led into worship, and my heart would gradually warm.

By the time I ascended the pulpit to preach, I was feeling at least that I was not completely dead. I labored to find some rhythm in my sermon and to keep everyone's attention. At some point, it seemed that someone else took over, and my mood and that of the congregation changed.

We were communing together before God. Not only were we not dead—we were very much alive. God had revived the preacher and people, and we became locked together before him and his Word. Lloyd-Jones aptly described this interaction among the Holy Spirit, the Word, the congregation, and the preacher:

> Another element to which I attach importance is that the preacher while speaking should in a sense derive something from his congregation. There are those present in the congregation who are spiritually-minded people, and filled with the Spirit, and they make their contribution to the occasion. There is always an element of exchange in true preaching. This is another way of showing the vital distinction between an essay and a lecture on the one hand, and a preached sermon on the other hand. The man who reads his essay gets nothing from his audience, he has it all there before him in what he has written; there is nothing new or creative taking place, no exchange. But the preacher—though he has prepared, and prepared carefully—because of this element of spiritual freedom is still able to receive something from the congregation, and does so. There is an interplay, action and response, and this often makes a very vital difference.[7]

One of my favorite logical fallacies to point out is *post hoc, ergo propter hoc*, which means "after the fact, therefore because of the fact." Humans fall into this fallacy all the time. Many people have a strong belief in elemental causes of sickness. For example, someone gets wet, or is caught in a strong wind, or steps on a cold floor, and then gets a cold. In some minds, the rain, wind, or the floor was the undisputed cause of the illness.

Although I have never actually seen the little critters, I tend to believe more in the germ theory of sickness. I attribute my cold to the person on the airplane who did not cover his cough or the woman who sneezed and then shook my hand and kissed me on the cheek.

Historians always have to propose causes for effects, and sometimes they may be right, but they are often speculative, committing *post hoc, ergo propter hoc*. I cannot say why revivals break out in certain places at certain times. Christians are renewed in their faith and unbelievers flock to Christ.

Perhaps they were primarily in answer to prayer, or missionary efforts, or persecution. There is another possible factor—extemporaneous preaching. I hasten to add that I do not know in which direction the causality runs. What is certain is that times of revival correspond to times of powerful extemporaneous preaching, but it is not clear which one is the cause and which one is the effect.

What follows are examples of correlation, leaving open the question of the direction of causality. All I can say is that this correlation appears in the history of the church and in my own experience. There are two possibilities, that revival produces extemporaneous preaching and that extemporaneous preaching produces revival.

Revival Produces Extemporaneous Preaching

We considered Archibald Alexander's delivery method in Chapter 3. He was a prime example of an extemporaneous preacher produced by a revival. James Garretson reported:

> It was during this year that the Rev. William Graham, who also served as Archibald's pastor, invited Alexander and several other students to accompany him in preaching engagements south of the James River and in congregations east of the Blue Ridge. Beginning in 1788, a number of congregations had begun to experience visitations of the Spirit; conversions were becoming more common and congregations were quickened to new levels of fervour and devotion in their service to the Lord.[8]

During that preaching tour, Alexander came under great conviction of his sin, and he gained some hope of his salvation. Not long afterward, in 1789, he made his public profession of faith in Christ and received communion. In 1790, Alexander began studying for the ministry under Graham, and he extemporaneously delivered his first public exhortation.[9] As I related in Chapter 3, Alexander described the experience as something that astonished him and his hearers, not as an effect that he could take credit for producing. Also, as already noted, he very rarely used any delivery method in the pulpit during his subsequent six decades of ministry except the extemporaneous one he had first discovered during that season of revival.

Another wider example comes from nineteenth-century Switzerland. In his installation discourse as Professor of Practical Theology in the Academy of Lausanne in 1837, Alexandre Vinet called the revival of his day a "movement" and announced the theme of his speech:

> It is incontrovertible that a movement has taken place in the sphere of religious things. The complaints of some, the congratulations of others, the interest of all, bear witness to this movement; and as we are among those who are thankful for it, the question… resolves itself naturally into this: What has preaching received from the religious movement, and what in return can preaching give to it?[10]

Referring to the revival also as an "awakening," Vinet defined it as "a reaching forth of christianity towards its source, towards a more comprehensive view of the evangelical system, towards a more exact and extensive application of christian principles to human life."[11] While stating that preaching was the way the movement was communicated, Vinet denied that preaching caused it because it was nothing truly novel but simply a deeper apprehension and practice of the Christian faith.[12]

However, he did note that the awakening had made preaching "more thoroughly Biblical."[13] He described this change:

> This profound respect, this reverence for the inspired Word, has made it literally to abound in our pulpits from which it had before descended only in drops. The sermon has more frequently been replaced by the homily, the paraphrase; explaining holy scripture, and, as much as possible, explaining it by itself, appears to be, as it was in the first days of the Church, the more immediate mission of the preacher; the gospel flows in full tide in our churches, enlivening at once

the eloquence of the minister and the interest of his hearers; the most insensible are made to feel the charm of his perpetual novelty; prejudice itself often expires before the divine unction of the Word; its sternest asseverations give less offense than our most prudent discourses; and preaching, as penetrated with this fresh savor, appears to gain equally in tenderness and authority.[14]

In other words, preaching became more expository as the preachers sought above all to communicate the Scriptures to their hearers. Preaching also became more evangelistic, no longer presupposing that the hearers needed only to grow in their faith but inviting them to believe in Christ in the first place.[15] Along with these changes, preaching grew more colloquial and less formal.[16]

Interestingly, preachers also suddenly became more extemporaneous in their delivery. Vinet reported:

From the multiplicity of oratorical exercises, in season and out of season, extemporizing proceeds, a practice which had been almost unknown among us. It even becomes necessary to those of our ministers who desire that religion amongst and around them should assume the character of a reality, and who cannot be content that a living word should exist only in a word recited.[17]

The awakening in Vinet's day transformed manuscript reciters into extemporaneous preachers.

James Alexander went so far as to generalize from such examples that revivals *always* produce extemporary preachers:

> Revivals of religion always train up off-hand speakers. It was my privilege to be early acquainted with the late Dr. Nettleton. I heard him preach in most favourable circumstances in Pittsfield, four-and-thirty years ago, and again at two later periods. Though one of the most solid, textual, and methodical speakers, he usually laid no paper before him. His speaking in the pulpit was exactly like his speaking by the fireside. I introduce his name for the purpose of reciting his observation that, in the great awakenings of Connecticut, in which he laboured with much amazing results, he scarcely ever remained in any parish of which the minister did not acquire the same extemporaneous gift.[18]

According to Alexander, extemporaneous preaching was as contagious as the revival itself, both being gifts of the Holy Spirit.

Extemporaneous Preaching Produces Revival

In terms of percentage of growth, there has likely never been a revival as great as the one that took place in the first century during the days of the apostles and their successors. Through Peter's first sermon, the church grew by 2500 percent. The sermons we have in the book of Acts make it clear that the apostles and their associates preached extemporaneously. Even so, the evidence is skewed toward evangelistic sermons preached on unplanned occasions, since we do not have a record of how Paul preached regularly during his year and a half in Corinth or his three years in Ephesus. However, it is hard to imagine that the apostles and their companions chose a completely different method for regular instruction, and we need to remember that writing materials were not as abundant or economical as they are today. Likewise, it is difficult to conceive of Paul using a manuscript long enough to take all night to read (Acts 20:7–12), although that would explain why poor Eutychus fell so soundly asleep.

William G. T. Shedd fixed the direction of causation as extemporaneous preaching producing spiritual movements. He wrote:

> It was the preaching of Christ and his apostles, of many of the early Fathers, of Luther and the Reformers. And whenever any great movement has been produced, either in Church or State, it has commonly taken its rise, so far as human agency is concerned, from the unwritten words of some man of sound knowledge and thorough discipline, impelled to speak by strong feeling in his heart.[19]

In the very next paragraph, Shedd went on to urge ministers to "study the Bible with a closer and more penetrating exegesis" in order that "greater results would follow from their preaching." He thus identified exegetical, extemporaneous preaching as a primary cause of spiritual revival. Shedd closed his chapter on extemporaneous preaching with a rousing prediction that united exegesis, extemporaneity, and revival:

> [W]hen thorough learning and diligent self-discipline shall go hand in hand with deep love for God and souls; and when the clergy shall dare to *speak* to the people with extemporaneous boldness out of a full heart, full head, and clear mind, we may expect, under the divine blessing, to see some of those great movements which characterized the ages of extempore preach-

ing,—the age of the apostles, the age of the Reformers, the age of John Knox in Scotland, the age of Wesley and Whitefield in England and America.[20]

Symbiosis

In light of Shedd's reference to George Whitefield (1714–1770), it is convenient at this point to mention his preaching, especially his delivery method. Friend of John and Charles Wesley and minister in the Church of England, he preached extensively in England, Scotland, and Wales, and later in the American colonies as one of the principle protagonists of the Great Awakening that occurred in the years 1740–43.

In Britain, his preaching won admiration and provoked opposition. In his introduction to *Select Sermons of George Whitefield* entitled "George Whitefield and his Ministry," Church of England Bishop J. C. Ryle remarked, "The plain truth is, that a really eloquent, extempore preacher, preaching the pure gospel with most uncommon gifts of voice and manner, was at that time an entire novelty in London. The congregations were taken by surprise and carried by storm."[21]

However, most clergymen closed their churches to Whitefield because they considered him to be fanatical. So he took the unorthodox step of preaching to thousands gathered in the open air. Ryle opined, "The plain truth is that the Church of England of that day was not ready for a man like Whitefield. The Church was too much asleep to understand him, and was vexed at a man who would not keep still and let the devil alone."[22]

At the instigation of John Wesley in 1737, Whitefield moved to the American colony of Georgia to manage an orphanage. Over the next years, he stoked the flames of revival that had begun in Jonathan Edwards' Northampton, Massachusetts parish in 1734.[23] Whitefield's sermon delivery method was distinct from that of the majority of preachers in America. Historian Mark Noll explained, "Whitefield and his imitators did not read their sermons like most of the colonies' settled ministers of the early eighteenth century but declaimed them extemporaneously in order to maximize their power."[24]

It is important to note that Edwards was reading full manuscripts of his sermons at the time when revival came to his church, so we ought not to tie revival too closely to any delivery method. At the same time, he is also another example of revival producing extemporaneous preaching, since Whitefield's visit in 1740 influenced Edwards to start using only notes or outlines in his preaching.[25]

The accounts of Whitefield's and Edwards' preaching point in two directions. They suggest (along with Shedd) that extemporaneous preaching was a primary stimulus of revival, and (along with Vinet and James Alexander) that extemporaneous preaching was a result of revival.

Dabney's experience also points to a symbiosis between the two. After two years at Tinkling Spring, he lamented in a January 1849 letter to his mother:

> They listen to my preaching very attentively, and often with fixed interest; but it always feels to me like the interest of the understanding and imagination only, and not of the spiritual affections. My preaching seems to human eyes to be utterly without effect; bad for me, and bad for them.[26]

However, the following year, Tinkling Spring was visited by

a revival. Under those renewed spiritual conditions, Dabney wrote again to his mother on June 8, 1850:

> Now it is a delightful indulgence to preach. The congregation full, the listening intent and solemn, one's own mind roused and elevated, and the people catching up any portion of divine truth, as if it were most powerful eloquence (provided it be spoken with unction), it is no effort to preach and no trouble.[27]

The season of revival soon came to a close, but the church added thirty-three members that year.[28] By the time Dabney left Tinkling Spring to teach at Union, he had become a powerful preacher. Apparently Dabney's preaching both stoked the flames of revival, and the revival honed Dabney's expository, extemporaneous preaching.

Conclusion

In the days of tent meetings (and in some places still to this day), people talked of holding a revival as if it were something that humans could plan and execute. It is more accurate to speak of being held by a revival. If revival is a divine gift, the most important activity of the Church to promote one is to pray that God would send it. At the same time, Christians are neither quietists nor fatalists. We pray that God would act, and we act. We pray for God's work, and we work in his strength.

In addition to praying, what is the most important work we can do? Preach the Word. God may be pleased to revive our own hearts and send revival to his church as we read from our manuscripts, or he may warm, convince, and convert through extemporaneous preaching. It is more essential that we preach the Word and that we preach Christ (which are truly the same thing) than that we follow any certain method of delivery. At the same time, lessons from church history correlate, on the one hand, the experiences of preachers letting themselves loose under the Spirit's impulse in their careful exposition of the Word with, on the other hand, God sending times of refreshment and growth on his beloved church. Even if we cannot map out the causes and effects with exactitude, at the very least, the history of prayerful, expository, extemporaneous preaching encourages us to make the attempt. Lloyd-Jones concluded his lectures this way:

> What then are we to do about this? There is only one obvious conclusion. Seek Him! Seek Him! Seek Him! What can we do without Him? Seek Him! Seek Him always. But go beyond seeking Him; expect Him. Do you expect anything to happen when you get up to preach in a pulpit? Or do you say to yourself, "Well, I have prepared my address, I am going to give them this address; some of them will appreciate it, and some will not?" Are you expecting anyone to have a climactic experience? That is what preaching is meant to do. That is what you find in the Bible and in the subsequent history of the Church. Seek this power, expect this power, yearn for this power; and when the power comes, yield to Him. Do not resist. Forget all about your sermon if necessary. Let Him loose you, let Him manifest His power in you and through you. I am certain, as I have said several times before, that nothing but a return to this power of the Spirit on our preaching is going to avail us anything. This makes true

preaching, and it is the greatest need of all today—never more so. Nothing can substitute for this.[29]

Let's review what we have covered in this book. The Introduction emphasized that a sermon is a spoken event. Chapter 1 introduced, compared, and evaluated three approaches to sermon delivery, recommending the extemporaneous above reading and reciting. Chapter 2 considered the difficulty of preaching and the need for faith and prayer. Chapter 3 presented some of the best wisdom of the ages on delivery, and Chapter 4 offered recommendations about how to become better public speakers. Chapter 5 issued warnings about the common pitfalls of extemporaneous delivery and how to avoid them. Chapter 6 provided a brief historical overview of the relationship between extemporaneous preaching and revival.

The coming Lord's Day is even now bearing down upon us. Let us therefore study the text diligently, pray for God's power, and let ourselves loose as the Spirit guides us. We may stammer our way through yet another sermon, or we may experience unusual eloquence, but we will keep on trying to communicate God's Word to the people. As Lloyd-Jones encouragingly observed: "Any man who has had some glimpse of what it is to preach will inevitably feel that he has never preached. But he will go on trying, hoping that by the grace of God one day he may truly preach."[30]

May we truly preach.

———

Prayer for Preparing a Sermon by Philip Doddridge

Blessed God! You gave me a rational soul, and I depend on you entirely to empower every capacity you have given me.

I am not sufficient in myself; all my sufficiency is of you.

Now I enter this important work, and I want to be aware of my need for your gracious assistance. Keep me focused on the work ahead of me, I beg you. Do not let any vain or intruding thoughts break in or hinder me. Direct my mind to proper thoughts, and to the best way of arranging and expressing them.

Fire my heart with holy affection, that divine thoughts still warm from my own soul may more easily penetrate into the hearts of those who hear me.

Help me remember that I am not speaking to gain a reputation for eloquence, but that I am preparing food for precious and immortal souls, dispensing that sacred gospel which my Redeemer brought from heaven and sealed with his blood.

So direct me to make this sermon most useful for Christian edification. And grant me refreshment as I study, that it may be one of the most joy-filled tasks of my life. While I am watering others, may I be watered myself also, and bring forth daily more and more fruit, to the glory of your great name, through Jesus Christ. Amen.[31]

---

1. Lloyd-Jones, 71.
2. Dabney, *Sacred Rhetoric*, 234.
3. Dabney, *Sacred Rhetoric*, 32.
4. Lloyd-Jones, 70.
5. Carter G. Woodson, *The History of the Negro Church* (Washington, DC: The Associated Publishers, 1921), 97–98 (found in *Documenting the American South*, University of North Carolina at Chapel Hill, <http://docsouth.unc.edu/church/woodson/woodson.html>).
6. Charles Hodge, *The Biblical Repertory and Princeton Review*, 1849, 453–57.
7. Lloyd-Jones, 84.
8. Garretson, 10.
9. For a full account of these experiences, see Chapters 4–6 of James W. Alexander's *The Life of Archibald Alexander*.
10. Vinet, 480.
11. Vinet, 481.
12. Vinet, 485–86.
13. Vinet, 486.
14. Vinet, 486–87.
15. Vinet, 489–90.
16. Vinet, 491–92.
17. Vinet, 492.
18. Alexander, *Thoughts on Preaching*, 150.
19. William G. T. Shedd, *Homiletics and Pastoral Theology*, 1867 (London: The Banner of Truth Trust, 1965), 212.
20. Shedd, 213.
21. J. C. Ryle, "George Whitefield and his Ministry," Introduction of *Select Sermons of George Whitefield* (Carlisle: The Banner of Truth Trust, 1958), 17.
22. Ryle, 21.
23. Sydney E. Ahlstrom, *A Religious History of the American People* (New Haven: Yale UP, 1972), 282–87.
24. Mark A. Noll, *America's God: From Jonathan Edwards to Abraham Lincoln* (Oxford: Oxford UP, 2002), 76.
25. Samuel T. Logan, "Jonathan Edwards and the Northampton Awakening," *Preaching and Revival* (London: The Westminster Conference, 1984), 58.
26. Johnson, 110.
27. Johnson, 112.
28. Johnson, 114.
29. Lloyd-Jones, 325.
30. Lloyd-Jones, 99.
31. Robert Elmer, ed., *Piercing Heaven: Prayers of the Puritans* (Bellingham, WA: Lexham Press, 2019), 140.

Made in the USA
Middletown, DE
20 May 2022

65948336R00096